ROB FLAMMANG

Surrender, The Way Out

ISBN: 1-4392-6512-7
ISBN-13: 9781439265123

Surrender, The Way Out

*One man's story of addiction
through to the other side.*

Purpose of This Book

This is not intended as another story of the ravages of addiction and the seemingly impossible quest to break free and find peace in sobriety, although that is one component of this story. This is about one man's struggle to find purpose and value, which is a quest common to us all. *Surrender, The Way Out* is this journey made through the alleys and byways of addiction. What makes this book unique from most other literature on the subject is the reader is treated to the view through the eyes and psyche of the addict.

There are three basic truths about addiction that are made clear in these pages. Firstly, heart issues usher us into addiction, secondly, heart issues keep us in the addiction cycle, and thirdly, heart issues are what prepare us to leave our addiction for recovery.

As one who struggled with addiction for twenty-eight years— now having twelve plus years clean and sober—I believe this book will benefit and give hope to the struggling addict at whatever stage of the process they may find them self. This work will also greatly benefit family and friends of the addicted. This book is intended to give hope, help, and encouragement to all who read it.

There is a way out. Recovery is not as complex as it may appear. What is complex are the webs of dysfunction we have been immersed in and the mountain of wreckage that has accumulated along the way. It is for these reasons that the old adage "one day at a time" and the wisdom in it, is so essential to the recovering person and his or her loved ones. We did not get here overnight nor will we quickly make things right. As we surrender to God, it is He who will take us by the hand and lead us out of the madness into a place of peace and safety.

Contents

Introduction

Sadly, addiction has become an all-too-common occurrence in our day. This is my story, but could very easily be yours or someone you know and love. As you enter my world through these pages, expect to see yourself or your loved one. It is my hope that this work will give you insight into the addict's struggle.

My upbringing was very typical of a blue-collar middle-class home in the '50s and '60s. My dad worked for the Southern California Gas Co. and Mom stayed at home and provided a clean, warm, and nurturing home. Dad was loved and respected in our home and extended family. He was a rock, a model of integrity and consistency. Mom was the heart of our home. She was the nurturer and instructor, and most always patient. Mom was always willing to show my sisters, Deonn and Darlene, and me, what needed to be done, how it was to be done, and why it was to be done. In the way of domestic and social duties we were well versed and trained.

Mom and Dad seemed to be ideal parents, and I believe to this day, in this regard, I was blessed more than most. It is to them, I dedicate the pages of this book. This is in many ways their story too. They were like fish out of water, facing things they knew nothing about. They accompanied me down this trail that eventually brought me to a place of surrender. Their part was more akin to being inadvertently swept into the vortex of a tornado and not knowing what the landscape would look like, when and if, they survived the ride. Dad did not get to see the end product. Although, before he went to be with the Lord in

December of 1994, he did experience a window of sobriety I had just prior to the final end of my struggle on February 6, 1997. Mom, though, has been able to enjoy for many years the fruit of their prayers. She has always been my number one cheerleader. I am so grateful for Dad's love and support, and that he never gave me the thrashing I deserved. In so many ways, Dad modeled God's love and dealing in my life.

I

The Boy Inside

I was born Robert Thomas Flammang II (sounds pretty impressive) September 3, 1952, to Robert and Virginia Flammang Sr. in Visalia, California. It was Mom's desire, not Dad's, to name me after my father. There was an old family friend, in his fifties then, named after his father, who was still referred to as "Junior." Dad did not want that for me, so I am "the second."

Visalia is the county seat of Tulare County in one of the richest agricultural regions in the United States and the world. Although I didn't grow up on ag land we were surrounded by it. My dad grew up on a ranch and my step grandparents also had a farm. Grandpa Dean and Grandma Jesse were the parents of Dick Henry, Mom's first husband and my older sister Darlene's biological father. Dick lost his life early in the marriage when his truck was hit by a train. This left Mom, at nineteen, a widow and single mom; Darlene lost her father at three years of age. This occurred in 1940. Mom married Dad in August of 1941, just a few months prior to the December 7 attack on Pearl Harbor.

After the war Dad returned to Visalia where, in 1948, he and Mom purchased their new home two miles west of town. Ours was the second of many homes to be built in the area, many of which would have one-acre lots. In those days, and for many more years to come, we would have the Hyde Cattle Ranch to the east of us and the Bell Quarter Horse Ranch along our northern property line. There was Mill Creek a few blocks to the south and a pond for the Hyde Cattle Ranch to the east. Life was simple then. I could have never imagined in a million years what the coming decades would bring.

My earliest memory, vague as it is, is of a birthday party at Mooney's Grove Park in a special area designated for such events for young children. It was a fully equipped fenced-in playground with tables. I was, most likely, four years old. Another early event in my life was a conflict with Mom, which culminated in my leaving home. I packed a Tupperware bowl full of raw oatmeal—a treat for me then—mounted my tricycle, and sped off. I made it to the end of Hurley Avenue where I ran out of food. It was at this point I returned home. I am sure my entire journey was under Mom's watchful eye.

My childhood was a happy and carefree one, quite appropriate for the '50s and early '60s. My dad had a blue-collar job at the Southern California Gas Co. and Mom was a full-time homemaker. There were few frills, but we never went without. If we did, we kids were not aware of it. In 1960 (I was eight years old) Mom got a job as a nurse's aide at Kaweah Delta District Hospital on the night shift. Mom later returned to school to get her LVN. She opted not to pursue her RN. It was patient care, not administrative duties, she loved. I can attest to this and the seriousness with which she tackled every task. I learned to take only major (*will die without care*) injuries to Mom for treatment. She would poke and prod, scrub, scrape, and pick, and worst of all, I could need stitches or a tetanus shot from Dr. Cas (*Castiglione*).

There was absolutely nothing more terrifying to me than getting a shot of any kind for any reason. I can still remember the year we could forgo our yearly polio shots at the local National Guard armory and, in their place, received the vaccine on sugar cubes at the city college. Thank you, Jonas Salk, what a saint!

With this as my background it's a wonder I ever tried heroin, even more so that I could puncture myself as often as needed in order to locate increasingly fewer and harder-to-find, injection sites.

To look at me then, there was nothing to indicate that my life would hold anything but an average existence. Both parents were committed to each other and to their children. My relationships with my two sisters, Deonn and Darlene, were good.

When I was about eight years old, Darlene, my older (by fifteen years) sister, married and moved out. Now I was no longer the annoying little brother, but I was now the oldest at home, and Deonn's older brother. I was a good older brother. Being a year and a half older and a grade ahead in school I would attend parties and activities that Deonn would not. It was my regular practice to bring her something, some portion of what I received.

One common thread I have recognized in the lion's share of addicts and alcoholics I have known over the years is a sensitive and caring side. With some it may be harder and more difficult to detect. For many, the masks, the offensive and defensive behavior weave a complex protective barrier guarding a tender underbelly. I have found this to be true with a wide range of personalities, both in the throes of addiction and in a variety of recovery settings.

One other thing I have seen, and in recent years come to understand more clearly, and that is, that there is a level of woundedness that predates addiction. In my own case, I believed for years that getting clean and sober was the answer and the solution to all my troubles. Not until I got clean in 1997 did I slowly begin to realize there was more to be dealt with than just my addiction and all the wreckage that came with it. Although I believe I have a genetic predisposition to addiction, my original motivation to use was a result of my own spiritual and emotional deficiencies. There was an ever-present indefinable void in me along with a powerful sense of insecurity that predated my drug use. This lack, this missing element, affected my relationships with others and the way I viewed myself.

From the beginning I had difficulty learning in school. Seeing myself as stupid—and ugly because of my freckles—all combined to create the beginnings of a very difficult cup to drink. Insecurity breeds insecurity, so as a young teen in the mid-1960s when I discovered alcohol and drugs I believed that I had found the greatest thing since sliced bread. It took many years for me to recognize that there were hidden costs in the fine print.

My early years in school were difficult and set the course and tone for the years to come. Kindergarten was where I first began to struggle academically, if you could call it that. I believe I was one of the last kids in my class to learn to tie a bow. My first bow was not tied in school, but rather at home. It was on my bathrobe. My other struggle that in my mind set me apart and made me different, was my long struggle to learn to skip, not skip rope, just skip. We all had to skip around the room together. I wondered if I would ever get it. It is one thing to struggle privately, quite another to do so under the watchful eyes of your peers. It was in kindergarten where I first began to taste failure.

In first grade this same pattern continued. I was a bit young to start, but old enough. As a student I was very average, except when it came to reading. I just could not get any traction in this realm of academia. This had two immediate consequences. Firstly, this bled into other subjects where reading was required. Secondly, and probably most devastating, I was separated and put in a remedial reading group. This made it official. I was different, I was stupid, I was less than. At the end of that year it was determined that I would be held back and repeat first grade the following year. It was now not only official, but now my classmates knew it, the whole school knew it, my family knew it, and the world knew it. Most of all, I knew it.

From this point on I saw myself differently. I was on the outside looking in. Like the picture you see in old movies of the outsider walking alone down the street. As he passes by the well-lit houses and shops filled with activity he longs to go in and be a part of it, but knows he can't. Maybe someday, some way, he will fit and be welcomed, but until then walking alone will be his lot. It is at this point that I believe an unconscious quest began to regain the ground I had lost; I would search to be accepted and be seen as an equal. With the seeds of inferiority that had recently taken root, all my efforts would be overwhelmed, just as the kudzu vine overwhelms and chokes out everything around it. Interestingly, I understand now that this battle, this struggle, raged in me with the rest of the world paying little, or no, attention at all. To this day it is easier and less threatening for me to connect with those older or younger than it is to connect with my contemporaries.

There was a girl in my class named Elizabeth. She was noticeably taller than the other girls and most of the boys; she was also very stocky, fat for the standards of the day. Elizabeth would often be picked on, as is common for any kid that is in any way different. I found myself standing with her, defending her, and acting as a buffer. Although I was not outwardly treated as she was, inwardly I felt a kinship. There we were, two kids very different in many ways, but inwardly not fitting in, standing against the tide.

These events, and the effects they had on me, were the seeds that would affect my life's course in ways that could be seen only in retrospect. I would eventually find a place in the subculture of drugs and the madness that comes with it, while at the same time trying to maintain a place in polite society. I'm sure, more often than not, I was only fooling myself.

There seems to be, as we approach and enter junior high, this great sorting process that takes place. It resembles the processing of fruit that comes in from the orchard. Up until this point all the fruit grows together. Even though there are differences in the fruit, when you look closely it is still lumped together on the same tree and receiving the same care. When the fruit is harvested it is trucked to the packinghouse where it is tested, sorted, and graded. It is here that the seemingly subtle differences in the fruit are amplified and taken into account. The fruit is separated by size and grade. It is this sorting process that determines the fruit's destination. Some go for fine fresh table use; others bulk sale, and still others for canning, and lastly, the culls, the most flawed. These are collected and sent to be crushed for juice and the pulp goes for cattle feed, or to be spread back in the orchards. Not a pretty analogy for junior high, but that is how this writer sees it and how I experienced it.

It was from this point on I found myself as a cull. I kind of fit as a cull, I was accepted as a cull, I was not rejected as a cull. That was not my first choice. I wanted to be table quality fruit, but was rejected and ended up in the cull bin. My course was set. It was the thugs and hoodlums, the lower strata of the social food chain.

There was little pretense with this crowd. There was one exception and that was to be seen as tough. I wanted, and needed, to be seen as a tough guy, but I never really was. I'm sure to many I seemed to be, but I always knew the truth. As a point of truth and record I was a fraud. The image I attempted to portray was a shield, a mask, all to protect the sensitive, insecure boy inside.

2

Choosing a Path

It is the early shaping of a life that creates the framework whereby choices are made. The components are many, but genetic and environmental comprise the two primary categories. It is with these in mind, and then add a God-given free will, and you have an autonomous human being charting his or her course through life. As onlookers, we may watch with amazement and wonder and be thoroughly convinced that at some previous time in a person's history they must have bumped their head, and very hard at that. We all make choices based on, and drawn from, our personal history, our heritage, and our perception of it. Part of the purpose of chapter 1 is to give you a glimpse into those parts of me. As we go through the pages of my life you will see more. The point of this book is not so much what I did, and how I lived; that is but the backdrop. The focus here are the internal forces that make medicating oneself a good idea to begin with, and how it is these same issues that keep us captive to what becomes an addiction.

In fourth grade I moved from George McCann, a Catholic school, to Willow Glen, a brand new public school just a few blocks from our home. I could walk or ride my bike to school. I would now have the same school schedule and holidays as my friends in my neighborhood. I just realized, as I am writing this, the difference that made in my relationships in the neighborhood and in school. Going to school with the same kids I lived near and played with, I believe, made a big difference in my socialization. I began to fit in at a level that surpassed anything up to that point. I believe there were two factors at play here. Firstly, I was no longer going into town for school with kids I saw only at school, and secondly, I'm sure, was age.

I distinctly recall feeling as though a whole new world had been opened up to me. No longer was I the dumb kid. I, for the first time, was experiencing some success in school, academically and socially. The demands of public school were less stringent and the teachers did not rule with an iron hand as the nuns did at George McCann. I'm sure the difference in class size was also a factor—fifty kids at Catholic school and fewer than thirty in public school. I was in a new world, and loved it.

In spite of all that I've just described, the image that had been forged in my mind about who I was did not go away. It did, however, submerge for a time, like a stealth submarine, waiting to surface at a more opportune time. It would be just a few short years; it would be in junior high.

It was in seventh grade that the relationships and security of those three short years began to unravel. I was finding that I no longer fit in the mainstream. This is where the very subtle differences of the past few years began to be more pronounced, and distinctions and separations began to take place. This was a painful reality to face. Just a few years before, I had made it up from the lower rungs of the food chain, and now I was losing ground. Remember the scene from the movie *A Christmas Story* where Ralphie finally makes it up to Santa Claus at the top of the stairs after a long, long wait in line? He has but a few short moments with Santa before he is sent down the slide. Ralphie tries to prevent going down, wanting to stay with Santa a little longer, and then the unthinkable happens, Santa pushes him away with his boot and he and the elf laugh as Ralphie slides down, back to the starting point. That was me, no longer fitting or feeling welcome. Who could I hang out with, where would I fit, who would accept me? My old self-image was awakened from its short sleep.

Looking back, it was at this juncture in my life that I began charting a different life course. I began to see the duplicity and the social game playing of the social elite—what a term to be used to describe seventh and eighth graders! That was not going to work for me; I just wasn't wired that way.

I must say that, as a rule, over my lifetime there have been very few people I have been unable to get along with, one on one. What has disappointed and disgusted me is the chameleon-like behavior I have experienced with people. What I mean by that is this: a person behaving one way, one on one, and becoming someone very different in a group.

3

I Had Found My People

A t this point I began testing the waters with a new crowd. I seemed to fit fine and they were certainly different from the mainstream kids with whom I was becoming more and more disillusioned. These kids were not striving to excel in school or the preppy social scene; they smoked (cigarettes) and had a tough "screw you" attitude. I had found my people. I was generally seen as a good kid by those who knew me and I did have a sensitive and caring heart. On the other hand, I had always had a hidden dark side. I was willing to lie and deceive to get what I wanted. I guess, to be honest, the duplicity and dishonesty that repulsed me in others, was, in point of fact, resident in me. It may have looked different, but I was no better than they were.

It is amazing the insight available in retrospect if we will take an honest look. Apart from God-given insight, I, for the most part, am so blind to my own faults and flaws. I also now understand that they, as well as I, were beginning to navigate life and make choices based on their own history and heritage. A gift I have received in recovery has been the principle of extending the same grace and mercy to others that I would hope would be extended to me. In my fifties now, I have come to recognize, to some small extent, how clueless and devoid of understanding I have been for most of my life. I know I have hurt many people out of sheer ignorance.

I was finding a place with this new crowd. There have always been two sides to me: the good, compliant, virtuous side, and the dark side, selfish, deceitful, and rebellious. With my old crowd the good side of me was accepted, but the dark side had to be hidden. With this new group it was the opposite; the dark side was preferred and the good and virtuous side was seen as weakness, and so had to be guarded. This was a big shift, but unfortunately one that was not too difficult for me to make.

Over the next thirty years the dark side would be my home. I was never totally at home there, and there would be many periods in my life where I would reside in both worlds simultaneously. Living in both created major inner conflicts, both in morality and with identity. I never lost my center. I was brought up with good moral training and knowledge of God. I always knew where home was; I just didn't want to live there full time.

It was at this point I began to smoke cigarettes, before school at the bus stop and at home. My smoking was hidden; although Dad smoked (a pipe), it was not permissible for me to do so. Dad had smoked from the time he was eight years old. Growing up on the ranch, and with one of the crops Grandpa Frank grew being tobacco, Dad and my Uncle Jack learned to roll their own cigars and cigarettes. As a matter of fact, Mom's first encounter with Dad was at a family friend's home; there were Dad and Jack, seven and eight years old, smoking their cigars. Mom was not impressed, and if my memory serves me, was warned away from them. There were folks who didn't believe "those Flammang boys" would live to see adulthood, and it wasn't because they smoked. They were the quintessential wild farm boys.

As a kid we would, from time to time, go camping in the Sequoia National Forrest. The highlight of the day for me was sitting around the campfire in the evening after dinner and listening to Dad tell stories about his life. This time with him was like looking through a window and getting a glimpse of an unseen part of my father.

Both Dad and his brother Jack were well known in the community but as adults were recognized for different reasons. Uncle Jack was a "hell-raiser." He was discharged as unsuitable for the Navy, enjoyed and had a lot of guns, pinup pictures of naked women on the walls of his den, and naked women tattooed on his arms. He was also a very heavy drinker and rode a Harley. One Saturday, shortly after my first fight, Uncle Jack brought out and presented me with a set of brass knuckles. I was thrilled, but Dad quickly put the kibosh on that. I was very disappointed and saw Dad as a square. In later years when I went to road camp to serve time on a burglary conviction, many of the guards, road crew bosses, and others recognized my name because they knew Uncle Jack. Dad, on the other hand, was a different story. In spite of Dad's wild upbringing he had a good heart. He was responsible and took care of business. I grew up being the beneficiary of his good character, but did not truly appreciate it until I reached adulthood.

Probably the greatest commentary on the life of my father was his funeral. As Mom and I and our family approached the gravesite for the graveside service I was upset because it was evident that another service had been scheduled for the same time right next to Dad's. As we got closer I realized that was not the case at all, all those people were there for Dad. These were all people that I knew and recognized as being a part of Dad's life. Just as you can read a man's checkbook and learn what he values, it's a man's funeral that will tell you the rest of the story. I have always been proud to have Dad as my father, but from that day on I have been honored to be recognized as the son of Robert Flammang Sr.

My life, and the way I have lived it out, has been a blend of Uncle Jack and Dad. For the past ten and a half years, as of the writing of this manuscript, I have consistently lived the life of my Father.

Adolescence is the time in our lives where we begin to chart our own life course. Up to this point, and I'm speaking in general terms now, we walk the course and hold the values of our family. It's at this point, as we begin taking steps of independence, that we also discard, or challenge, some long-held adopted values and experiment with the values and world views of the new people of influence making their way into our lives. The scary thing here is that this is all happening at a time when there are other major changes taking place. Our bodies are changing, our hormones are raging, and our brains are actually changing in the way they operate. What a time to start venturing out.

So draw together the components of this chapter and you have a gangly adolescent that was losing his newly won, short-lived place in the social food chain, with his good-self and bad-self waging war for supremacy. Add to that a changing body, raging hormones, and a brain whose wiring was actually being altered by the growth process. With all this in mind I was beginning to make life choices. Scary, ha!

4

The Long Fork in the Road

It was now my freshman year in high school. Looking back, the course I took was a process. In fact, it was not even planned. It would be like leaving Boston Harbor with a course set for Liverpool, England, and, once setting sail, never again referring to the navigational charts to check position and make course corrections to allow for winds and currents. To do so would bring you to land off the coast of South Africa. That is a picture of my life course. Other than wanting to do well in life I had no direction, no plan. Not that I didn't want one. I responded to the winds and currents of life as they came, with no real direction other than to stay out of trouble, or should I say, not get caught.

At this point in life, although Mom and Dad were present, I kept them out. I was navigating emotionally and intellectually alone. I was on my own, and felt it.

It was 1968 and the winds of Haight Ashbury were making their way from San Francisco into the San Joaquin Valley. These winds affected clothing styles, hair length, and attitudes about everything from politics to sex. This was the "Age of Aquarius," a time when sex, drugs, and rock and roll swept through the youth and college cultures like a giant tsunami. In the San Joaquin Valley, the heart of California, and a bastion of conservative thought and tradition, resistance was strong, and change slow and grudging, but, as with all tsunamis, the immovable is moved and the unchangeable is altered.

This was a difficult time for the establishment but an exciting time for the young. This could be compared to surfers riding a tidal wave with all the thrill and excitement that provides, but all the while having no clue as to the devastation to come. It was this period that energized and accelerated my journey down the road of a drug driven life. "Better living through chemistry" was my mindset.

High school was a big foreboding place. The campus was sprawling and unfamiliar, the crush of unfamiliar faces was intimidating and played on each and every insecurity and self-doubt that was a part of the psyche of this adolescent. As I clung to the familiar faces from junior high my circle of acquaintances gradually widened. It was in this broadening circle, through which the influences that would shape my future, entered.

The social and cultural landscape of high school was more complex and defined than junior high. The groups were as follows:

The "Soches" were the social upper crust.

The "Jocks" were the football players and cheerleaders.

The "Cowboys" were agies, or goat ropers, as we called them.

The "Chicanos" were the Hispanics.

The "Hippies," were a very small group just forming; this was 1968.

Lastly, were the "Hardasses," of which, I was a part. We were a group of academic and social underachievers. We smoked, drank, used drugs, and fought. I excelled when it came to getting loaded, but, as a tough guy, any image I had was derived more from association than from any real action on my part. As a side note, our group was infiltrated by two young-looking undercover cops, as I came to recognize later. This was very uncommon in those days.

It was here that I began to develop coping mechanisms: how to medicate my emotions and the very slow and painful process of developing effective masks to shield a very sensitive Rob. This process, over the next twenty-eight years, was honed and refined, continually reassessed and adjusted each time there was a breach in my defenses or I felt pain of any sort. Eventually my walls were so thick and so high that I began to feel the pain of my own isolation. Walls intended to protect also imprison. In the latter years of my addiction I took great pride in how little I felt. After many, many years the young tenderhearted boy had emerged a man with the heart of stone. To be more accurate, it was a stone cap, with that still sensitive heart buried underneath. I believe the hardest of people, as a rule, are among the most wounded.

My interest in school was in theory only. I understood that an education was necessary to do well, and I did want to do well and succeed in life. I could find no direction or interest to pursue, even though I met with guidance counselors. Scholastically I never got traction. With no specific goal or objective, I floundered in the sea of mediocrity. I believe this floundering fueled the fires of low self-worth and insecurity that by then had burned in me for years.

I was a train wreck just waiting to happen, with all these elements converging at one point. The emerging drug culture had my answer; the solution was clear, "better living through chemistry," or the other mantra of the era "there's hope with dope." This was easy and felt good. Let's party!

For this adolescent, I had found the greatest thing since sliced bread. All was well with Rob, and the world, when I was loaded. This also solved another issue. I now had purpose, and my purpose was to feel good. For the first time in memory I felt comfortable in my own skin, I didn't feel inferior.

Initially I was a weekend warrior, but in a relatively short space of time my drug use would develop into a full-time endeavor. Unlike my contemporaries who used recreationally, drugs quickly became a way of life. The relational landscape of my life changed accordingly. I began to connect more and more with those who used as I did, hard-core users, and I fit less and less with social users.

5

Finding Purpose

When I was about seventeen, a couple of buddies and I went to score heroin. We picked up an old "veterano." This guy had been a dope fiend for decades; he knew the ropes and had good connections. We pulled up to a tiny run-down house out in the country. He got in the front seat, I was in the back, and we took off to the nearby town of Farmersville where he would score for us. I remember being impressed that he had money for dope and didn't work. Being young and inexperienced I struggled to get dope money each day. I remember sitting in the backseat watching and listening to this guy and seeing him as a success, not really noticing the run-down house he lived in and the fact that he didn't have a car. I said to myself that day in the backseat, "I want to be able to do that, have enough money for dope and not have to work."

I now had purpose and I now had a goal, twisted as it was. I can tell you now, that after years of learning the ropes and being driven hard by the demons of addiction, I reached my goal. But, like many goals, what waits for us as reward when we attain them, is not what we imagined.

Back at school, in my sophomore year, the dean of boys and I had a meeting. Mr. Scott presented the idea that I transfer to continuation school; he felt I would do better there, and so did

I. Continuation was where all the troublemakers and misfits were sent in an attempt to, at least, keep them in school. I realize now, had I not agreed, I would have at some point ended up there anyway. The move for me was great. I would be required to be in school only from 8:30 to noon. This meant more time and fewer obstacles standing in the way of fulfilling my purpose and attaining my goals, "better living through chemistry," and its financing.

It was about this time I began dealing drugs. It was small scale, nothing fancy. What I found was unexpected. Dealing helped finance my activities but it also elevated me socially. I was somebody now, people sought me out, and there was power and influence, even dealing on a small scale.

6

A Life Consumed

From this point on it was all about drugs, the using and acquisition, and everything that went with that.

I must interject and point out here that I, out of necessity, was living a double life. I had to maintain appearances to avoid family and legal conflicts. This was something I would carry on into adulthood and into my first two marriages. This meant intercepting the mail to alter report cards before Mom and Dad saw them. This meant forging notes to the school explaining my absences, and altering odometers on cars to disguise actual miles driven. Also included, was alerting friends that my Dad and I sounded a lot alike on the phone. And this does not even begin to touch on the avoiding, disguising, and lying to cover the drug use. Living a lie necessitates keeping people at a distance; this also in turn isolates.

Our home was very conventional for the time, no drinking (by minors) and absolutely no drug use was permitted. I even had great difficulty letting my hair grow long—which, at that time, was representative of the emerging cultural shift. Any trouble, or grave misstep on my part, was used as leverage and occasion to force a haircut. I remained hopeful, although I wondered if I would ever have long hair. For me this was about the desperate struggle for identity and finding my place; fitting in. For Mom and Dad it represented rebellion and a culture they recognized as harmful.

Like most addicts, the addiction is constant and continual, but the vehicle, or drug of choice, may vary over time. It was methamphetamine that accompanied me across the line from recreational user to addiction. My use was extreme, even for an addict. "Beans," as we called them, were small round tablets about the size of a baby aspirin and had a cross scored on the face, also known as "cross tops." These were pharmaceutical grade, much superior to the methamphetamine of today.

Most recreational users would take one or two, maybe four or five; my dose was fifty a day, preferably all at once—on a really good day it could be twice that. This level of use severely twisted my thinking and behavior. My weight plummeted to 120 pounds on a six foot one inch frame, and sleep was greatly limited. In keeping with the web of deceit necessary to maintain my addiction I was able to deflect concern over my gaunt frame, and my constant peering out of windows.

It was in this state that I, in crafts class, came close to mangling my hand on a table saw. It was at this point Mr. Burris, the principal, stepped in. He, like Mr. Scott in another meeting, felt my needs could be better served elsewhere. He suggested I "get help." In those days no one was sure what that looked like. This was all happening at the beginning of a new drug epidemic and no one was sure how to address it—not the medical, psychological, legal, or spiritual communities. Many things have been tried over the years, most with good intentions, but with limited and somewhat short-lived success. Regarding Mr. Scott and Mr. Burris, I respected them both and I believe they wanted to see me do well. I had the same relief leaving continuation school as I did regular high school.

I must repeat that the focus of this book is not to chronicle the sordid details of addiction; to do so would only add to the volumes already written on such matters, but my intent is to lay out this man's journey of "coming to the end of himself." So with that in mind we continue.

My family had gotten acquainted with a pastor who had a heart for addicts. Doug had moved from Fresno, where he had worked with addicts and those from that culture, as part of Teen Challenge. My parents loved him and his wife, Marilyn, and their three boys. Doug and Marilyn embraced the addicted, the criminally inclined, and their families. In turn, our community embraced them. We were a small town with big problems. Mom and Dad were but two in a sea of parents, school officials, law enforcement, and those from the medical community who were desperately searching for answers; Doug knew the terrain and seemed to have some answers. Doug was the driving force, and with the support of my parents, and many others like them from our community, he founded "Turning Point," a residential recovery program, the first in our community.

I recall one Christmas Mom and Dad having all the residents and some staff of the program over for dinner and a festive evening. The only detail I recall was drinking Bacardi 151 rum and Coke and thinking I was being discrete. I'm sure everyone could smell it and I always drank to get a healthy buzz. Why someone didn't just jerk me out of there I'll never know. The lack of appropriate action taken in that setting, I believe, was indicative of the time. No one really knew what to do. This was a time of learning for everyone. Those who seek treatment today are the beneficiaries of these early treatment pioneers.

It was Doug who directed us to my first rehab program, it happened to be in Santa Cruz, California.

7

Off to Rehab

I was eighteen and I was a mess, sucked up and squirrely. At
120 pounds, you could just about count my teeth with my
mouth closed. As Mom and Dad drove me north through the
valley and then west through the hills, I had no idea where I
was going, much less what to expect. My only travel experience
to this point had been camping in the Sequoias or vacationing
in Cayucos, a small blue-collar vacation spot on the coast of
California, and a few other spots. Now I was going to a place I
didn't know, and would be left there—sounds like a kid going
to camp. This was no camp.

We arrived, pulling up to the old county hospital in Santa
Cruz. It was now occupied by an eclectic group of recovering
addicts, some with their families, who had become Christians.
This was around the time of the big "Jesus movement" that swept
the nation and the youth culture. I still remember a nice 1954
Cadillac parked out front. I had one just like it, but not as clean.
They were expecting me. We met with the assistant director, and
then Mom and Dad said their good-byes.

I was taken to a long room on one end of the large one-story
L-shaped building. This room seemed to be all windows, as if
it had been a sunroom at one time. What a place for a hyper-
vigilant speed freak to be put. It was there, in one of the many

beds lined up like ducks, where I slept for the next three days, opening my eyes secretively from time to time to observe my new surroundings.

The other people there were all from my world but they were from very different parts of it. At eighteen I was the youngest, other than a few children who lived there with their parents. There was an American Indian in his fifties, quiet and contemplative; a white tough guy lowrider and his wife from Los Angeles. There was a gal about ten years older than me, who had been a prostitute—we talked a lot, she was nice. This place was a menagerie of backgrounds and personality types. The one thing we all had in common was the destructive force of addiction.

Addiction, its causes, and the wreckage it brings, is complex to treat. There are many approaches to treatment and these vary. The same premise for treatment can be presented differently from program to program. There are some universal truths about addiction, but there is no "one size fits all" when it comes to treatment. What I am about to say may seem contradictory. There are many approaches to treating addiction, but I believe there is only one solution. It is my hope that this conclusion will be borne out in the pages of this book.

The destructiveness and bondage of addiction were addressed simply in this program. God can and will free you if you give yourself to Him. I'm not sure if that was actually said to me or not but that was what I understood.

The Center was supported by donations and a large thrift store. Everyone had a job and tasks to accomplish. In the evenings we would have a Bible study at the Center, or we went to the thrift store for what resembled a church service in one end of the very large building. It was a nice setting.

My addiction had taken its toll. I was left physically, mentally, and emotionally depleted. I had been "rode hard and put away wet." I had come to a place I'd never been before. I had "hit bottom." I felt so alone, so spent and used up.

One evening, at one of the church-like meetings at the thrift store, something happened. I found myself up front with my face in my hands, with no prompting or direction from anyone. I was broken, asking God if He was real to please help me and forgive me. After some time I got up; something was so different. I felt as though a massive load had been lifted from my shoulders. Whatever this was, it was good. I knew nothing of theology, and my Catholic upbringing had not prepared me for what was taking place. I have never been given to emotion. This was not emotion, although strong feelings of relief and peace were now present, where before there had only been loneliness, anxiety, and grief. I knew one other thing, "me and God were cool." For the first time in my life I wasn't in fear of going to hell. Prior to that I never knew where I stood with God. I believed my best shot at heaven would be for me to be killed immediately after confession. I would have no time to sin.

A few days later something else began to happen. You know the cartoons we see of an angel on one shoulder and the devil on the other, both whispering opposing arguments for your loyalty and a course of action. This began to happen to me. No one explained it to me but it was clear what was happening. I remember feeling like a wishbone with God on one side and Satan on the other. This was horrible. I didn't know how to fight this. I kept this battle to myself and in so doing I'm sure I sealed my fate. In nature, elk and caribou find safety in the herd. Predators seek out stragglers, or will isolate an animal from the protection of the herd where they can more easily take them down. Looking back, I see my own insecurities isolated me and I began to withdraw.

Many things contributed to the buildup. Finally one day, at our weekly car wash, I reached my breaking point. A big white lowrider Cadillac pulled in and out stepped four guys in motorcycle boots, greasy Levis, and motorcycle chains. These guys represented everything I was, and wanted to be, and now I was with all these squares, these sissy Christians. I was done, that was the last straw, I was out of there. I went to the guy in charge and told him I was done. I walked eight or nine miles back to the Center, packed my suitcase, and caught the next Greyhound bus home. The tug of war was over.

Again relief, I could now go back to my people, to what I knew. I wasn't going to use, I'd had enough, I'd stay clean!

8

What Now?

I 've been to rehab. Now what? I'm no longer strung out and I've had a very real encounter with God. What do I do now? I didn't have a problem with God, but I didn't want to be a square for Jesus. The only appealing place to turn, and all I knew was the old crowd, I just wouldn't use. That lasted maybe two weeks.

Recovery is far more than not using. Authentic recovery is going beyond physical sobriety and addressing the underlying issues that make using a viable option. It is only as these things are recognized, and addressed, that we can begin to develop emotional sobriety. Physical sobriety is a prerequisite to attaining emotional sobriety.

Recovery is a process, and reaching a point of surrender is also a process. Surrender is on the other side of bottom, and ground zero is the last thud in a long series of bottoms. In an old Laurel and Hardy scene, Stan and Ollie were sitting at the dinner table. There was a loud commotion above them, and then people and furnishings came crashing down on them from above, causing the floor they were on to collapse. This in turn, caused a chain reaction that continued down through several stories and ended with a thud in the basement. In the addiction process we continue to dig new and deeper bottoms if we persist, causing and accumulating more and more wreckage as we fall further and further, deeper and deeper. Bottom is when we put our shovel down, or die in the process.

In the early years of my addiction my greatest handicap was my youth—young, dumb, and bulletproof. I could recuperate quickly, do things differently next time, and there were always codependent family and friends around to soften the consequences and repair the wreckage of my behavior.

So, now that I've done rehab, I'm off again. I won't let things get out of hand this time. Bear in mind, no addict sets out to get addicted and for a while does not recognize that he or she is, in fact, addicted. In the early days, I truly believed I could quit anytime I wanted; I just liked it too much to quit, kind of like potato chips.

As you read this account of my journey, bear in mind, there is no clean, crisp, chronological order. Many things overlap in the way they happened and in the memory of them. This is by no means meant to be a complete and concise account of my life experience; many events and activities have been left out by design. There are no years or dates to the events in these pages, but I do believe I've got the general order correct. Much of my experience is no longer accessible to clear memory and many things that are, I would rather were not. One other point to make here is that the physical, or outward journey, is not the central point to this story, but it is the internal process, shaped by the external, that is the focus of this writer.

What brings change is my focus. It was the internal that fueled my addiction and it was, in turn, the external addiction that prepared me internally for change. My inner woundedness made drugs a good idea and it was my addiction that brought me to the One who could heal my wounds. For this reason alone, my years of addiction were worth it. "It takes what it takes."

I came to the end of myself on the outside, not on the inside, many, many times. You may have heard the account of a boy being corrected and disciplined by his father. The boy is made to sit in the corner for a length of time. The boy is determined to have his way and stands up. The father physically sits him down. The boy continues to stand and the father continues to sit him down. The boy finally stops getting up, but looks at his father and says, "I may be sitting down on the outside, but I'm standing up on the inside." It took me twenty-eight years to sit down on the inside.

So now, after about a six-week respite in rehab, I was back home. I was well rested and had gained some weight. I also had a new awareness of God I didn't know what to do with. I wanted to do well, to be happy and successful, but I was still the same inside. I was still terribly insecure, desperately needing to be accepted, and fearful of rejection. Inside, I was still lost and alone, so I picked up where I left off with the old crowd. I continued doing what I knew how to do, and that was to medicate my fears and insecurities.

Prior to this point I had been arrested twice for DUI (driving under the influence). Back then it was referred to as a "502." Our home was also raided and a search warrant served. My room and car were searched. I escaped arrest by the skin of my teeth. I had just sold the last of the drugs I had been dealing before returning home. Needless to say, Mom and Dad were not happy. Mom told me years later that as my room was being searched, she stood at the top of the stairs going down to my room, telling the detectives, "But he's a good boy, he's a good boy." Mom's denial surrounding my addiction and behavior over the years exceeded my own. She regularly rescued me from the consequences of my addiction and poor choices. Dad was upset and his response was to order me to get a haircut. I didn't want to do that, and I also knew I was in deep trouble and that was probably just the beginning, so I left the house as if to comply with Dad's demands and didn't come back. I eventually did return weeks later when things had cooled down. Mom was frantic and concerned for my safety, so she was relieved to have me home, and Dad, I'm sure with Mom's help, had cooled off and allowed me home.

A fact about addiction is that it gets progressively worse, never better. So with that in mind my prospects didn't look good, but I was different, I was in control. I knew nothing of the inevitable worsening grip of addiction. My addiction blinded me to the evidence of my true condition that was all around me, accidents, deaths, and friends going to jail and to prison. I would not let these things happen to me, that was them, I would be careful.

I continued to use meth but began to gravitate to heroin. Heroin numbed and satisfied my inner demons in ways meth couldn't. There is a gorilla that takes hold of you that is quite different than the taskmaster that comes with meth.

Things progressed and I found myself facing a felony burglary charge; I was nineteen. I was convicted at trial, but was sentenced as a juvenile; I was only eighteen at the time of the offense with no prior convictions. I received a lenient sentence of four months and probation to follow. I was sent to road camp to serve my time, I was glad I got an adult facility. There I met guards, road crew bosses, and inmates who knew my family, in particular, Uncle Jack. Things went as well as could be expected. I was able to continue to drink and use while there. I was attacked once when another inmate tried to tell me what to do and I blew him off. Then with two days to release, and a "homecoming" party in place, I lost my "good time credit" for a dangerous and foolish stunt on the road crew. I got no more visits from family after that. They were upset, and they ate my cake. There was no cake when I did come home.

This arrest and jail time was a wake-up call. Not about drugs, but about how and with whom I did the things I did. From that point on I weighed more carefully the risks I took. I found going solo gave me more control at managing risk and I did not have to share the rewards. The actual drug use is only part of the equation for the addict. The other part is the getting, and all that that entails. Thefts, lying, and manipulation are all part of the world of the addict. Drugs and crime are inseparable; they truly do go hand in glove.

Part two of my burglary conviction was probation. That meant a leash and a watchdog. My probation officer was on me like "white on rice." I had a friend who had the same probation officer and he was left alone. I, on the other hand, got regular visits from Bill. He not only came by, but he took me for coffee. This was not looking good for me, or to the people who saw me with him in his car. This caused my loyalty to be brought into question. I came to recognize later this was because he saw hope for me, where he didn't in others.

I continued to use, and did some dealing, trying not to get nailed. "If it looks like a duck, and quacks like a duck, it probably is a duck." Bill finally gave me a choice: jail, or a program. I'd tried both and so opted for another program. I had no interest in change, just avoiding jail, so we tapped the services of Doug once more. He was the pastor who worked with street folks and addicts and had directed me to my first rehab program in Santa Cruz.

Soon I found myself in a car, with Doug, heading to Los Angeles. We pulled into the driveway of a large two-house property about a mile from UCLA. This place was run by a Lutheran minister and his wife who had a heart for messed-up young people. It was basically run like a very large family, with the girls in one house, and the guys in the main house, with Allen and Eunice, as we called them.

The program consisted of Bible studies, church on Sunday, and everyone had chores. It was pretty lax, and you could easily get away with a lot. I wanted a better life and I began to see this as an opportunity. My encounter with God at my first program seemed to prepare me for this one. I was finding things here that built on what had taken place a couple of years earlier. This was very quickly becoming a good thing. There seemed to be a sense of order in all this.

There was a young college coed who helped Allen and Eunice with secretarial skills and oversight responsibilities. We became good friends and in time got married. Her father was not pleased; her mother was a little more accepting.

I did not leave the program with a firm grasp on sobriety. I was still drinking some. But, I did have a better understanding of God, and a wife. Seemed like forward movement to me.

We settled on making Santa Barbara our home after trying Visalia for one summer. The heat was difficult for Lene *(Danish: pronounced Lena)* and Santa Barbara was where she grew up and had family. I loved the coast and that made it heaven. In time, hell would catch up with me.

9

Am I Different Yet?

I was now a husband, a head of household. I would also soon be a father. We got pregnant right away. I was in shock. We were living with my parents and had not as yet determined where we would settle. We were a young couple ill prepared for the step into marriage we had just taken, much less parenthood. I did not have a job and we did not have a place of our own yet. Children were not even on my interest list at this point.

As the shock wore off, I very slowly began to warm up to the idea until my excitement matched my wife's. By the end of term, I could hardly wait. When Angela was born I was in heaven. I even changed diapers, wet and dirty. I took her for walks, carrying her in her backpack, and danced with her each morning before I went to work. She meant the world to me. My addiction would eventually exert such overwhelming influence over me that I would risk, and eventually forfeit, my marriage and the children I adored.

My life now centered around my family and church community. I had embraced a relationship with God and all that entailed. My commitment was genuine and was walked out with the same singleness of purpose as with my addiction. Although I was not using drugs, I struggled to refrain from drinking. I have always viewed alcohol as a drug and I agonized over my inability to remain totally clean and sober.

I believed my addiction was behind me and a thing of the past, and the drinking, at some point, I would get a handle on. The fact was, it was lying low, like a hungry lion waits and stalks its prey in the tall grass and its prey is unaware of the danger. I was unaware of the place my addiction still held in my life. It was not gone at all; it had just changed its spots, and at this point, was quietly biding its time. I had quit, but my surrender to God had some holes in it.

There are many levels of surrender. In war, a soldier is overpowered and surrenders. If, while in the POW camp, the soldier begins to dig an escape tunnel he or she has surrendered only on the outside, not on the inside. In police actions there are different levels of surrender at the end of a pursuit.

There is the:

- Stop running, still standing, surrender
- Stop running, still standing, arms in the air, surrender
- Stop running, down on your knees, arms in the air, surrender
- Stop running, lying face down on the ground, surrender
- Stop running, lying face down on the ground, handcuff yourself, put yourself in the police car, plead guilty in court, willingly pay all costs for your offense, and make full restitution, surrender.

I was for real and serious about my new direction in life. What I have since come to understand is that the addiction battle is greater than I imagined. Quitting, as difficult as that may be, is actually the easy part. Most addicts you talk to will admit to quitting multiple times. It's the "staying quit" that is the hard part. It is at that point that all the internal reasons for using in the beginning, resurface and face you like a lion, lying in wait for its prey.

It is God's intent to walk us through a recovery process where our inner wounds and hurts can be addressed, as well as any other baggage we are dragging along. This process requires surrender, surrender to God. The first three of the "12 steps," in a nutshell, are: I can't, God can, and I'll let Him.

Surrender in my life has been a process, a long one at that. Over the years I have surrendered many, many times for different reasons and with various motives. Often the truth of my motivation was obscured, even from me. To use the police chase analogy; for years after my surrender, at whatever intermediate level that would be, I would get up and run again, my internal baggage spurring me on, never letting me rest. Sometimes knowing things would be no different than before, and at others, truly having hope; it would be different this time. This process has taken many, many painful years. I, for years, have had this picture in my mind of a determined mule, standing, and his owner in front of him, grasping a board with both hands, and the question being posed, "How many times is it going to take to get this mule to lie down, and not get up again?"

You may be wondering, what's the big deal about surrender. It has everything to do with humility, without which there is no recovery. Without genuine humility you will not come to God on his terms. Without God the most you will have is abstinence. Abstinence does not equal recovery. Without recovery there is no emotional sobriety or inner healing.

The following is a list of significant events on my road to recovery. It has been compiled over that last few years as my memory has rebounded. This list is by no means all inclusive or chronologically precise and is intended to help put my struggle into context. My story is my journey, as I remember it, and my perception of it. I know others may view my life differently and with a less sympathetic view; it is a matter of vantage point.

ROB'S ROAD TO SURRENDER

	Age	Event	Location
I.	16	Arrest, DUI	Visalia
2.	16	Mental Health Group Therapy Two Years	Visalia
3.	17	Arrest, DUI	Visalia
4.	18	Narcotics Raid for Drug Dealing, No Arrest	Visalia
5.	18	Suicide Attempt, Cut Wrists	Visalia
6.	18	Recovery Program, DAPC	Santa Cruz
7.	18	Met God	Santa Cruz
8.	18	Hepatitis AB	Visalia
9.	19	Arrest, Felony Burglary	Visalia
10.	19	Drug Overdose	Visalia
11.	20	Recovery Program, Renewal House	Los Angeles
12.	20	Drug Overdose	Los Angeles
13.	20	Marriage No. I	Santa Barbara
14.	23	Antibuse Treatment	Santa Barbara
15.	26	Separated from Wife No. I	Santa Barbara
16.	26	Recovery Program, New House	Santa Barbara
17.	27	Arrest, restraining order violation	Santa Barbara
18.	27	Recovery Program, DAPC	Santa Barbara
19.	28	Recovery Program, New House	Santa Barbara
20.	29	Divorce No. I	Santa Barbara

21.	29	Treatment Program, Schick Shadel Hosp.	Santa Barbara
22.	29	Drug Overdose	Santa Barbara
23.	31	Methadone Detox	Tulare
24.	31	Recovery Program, TITLE	Visalia
25.	32	Drug Overdose	Visalia
26.	32	Methadone Detox	Tulare
27.	33	Recovery Program, TITLE	Visalia
28.	33	Hepatitis B	Visalia
29.	33	Trexan Treatment	Tulare
30.	34	Recovery Program, Victory Outreach	Visalia
31.	34	Marriage No. 2	Visalia
32.	36	Recovery Program, Victory Outreach	Visalia
33.	36	Recovery Program, Victory Outreach	Visalia
34.	36	Recovery Program, Victory Outreach	Visalia
35.	37	Recovery Program, Victory Outreach	Visalia
36.	37	Recovery Program, Victory Outreach	Visalia
37.	37	Recovery Program, Victory Outreach	Bakersfield
38.	37	Recovery Program, Victory Outreach	Hanford
39.	37	Methadone Detox	Fresno
40.	38	Methadone Maintenance	Fresno
41.	38	Methadone Detox	Fresno
42.	38	Heroin/Trexan Reaction	Visalia

43.	38	Drug Overdose		Visalia
44.	39	Detox, Mill Creek Hospital		Visalia
45.	39	Recovery Program, Pine Recovery		Visalia
46.	39	Recovery Program, PARR Center		Porterville
47.	39	Arrest, Petty Theft, and Receiving		Visalia
48.	40	Recovery Program, PARR Center		Porterville
49.	40	Methadone Detox		Tulare
50.	40	Suicide Attempt, Pill Overdose		Visalia
51.	41	Recovery Program, PARR Center		Porterville
52.	42	Separated from Wife No. 2		Visalia
53.	42	Hepatitis C		Visalia
54.	43	Divorce No. 2		Visalia
55.	43	Methadone Detox		Fresno
56.	43	Methadone Maintenance		Fresno
57.	43	Methadone Detox		Tulare
58.	43	Treatment, Cedar Vista Hospital		Fresno
59.	43	Methadone Maintenance		Fresno
60.	43	Arrest, DUI		Visalia
61.	44	Detox, Cedar Vista Hospital	2/6/97	Fresno
62.	44	Treatment, The ARC	2/11/97	Reedley

2 Failed Marriages
6 Arrests
1 Narcotics Raid
2 Suicide Attempts
3 Hepatitis Episodes (AB, B, and C)
6 Drug Overdoses
20 Residential Program Stays
18 Clinical Treatment Processes

This Was a Twenty-Eight-Year Process.

This list of events, and its details, was pieced together over a ten year period of time from available documents and memory; it is by no means whole and concise.

Coming to the end of oneself is a process and the components of that journey differ for each one of us.

A friend once told me, "God can take the chapters of regret in our life and rewrite them into a story of grace." I have found this to be true in my life; I encourage you to allow it to become true in yours.

I will forever be grateful for the prayers of those around me that kept me safe from any serious harm.

10

Married With Children

Now I was a husband, and father of two girls. I was a responsible provider and an engaged and involved husband and father. My limited, occasional, drinking was an unwanted presence in our home by me and especially my wife. There was a coercive pull that eventually won out, and I drank, sometimes a little and sometimes much. This presence was my still-present addiction, making its presence and influences felt. I didn't want to give in; I wanted to be a regular guy.

My first job in Santa Barbara was as a parts fabricator in the nearby community of Goleta. Being indoors all day was difficult for me and in time I took a position working outdoors in landscape maintenance. I liked this much better and I seemed to have an aptitude for it. This eventually led to a job on a large estate in the very exclusive community of Montecito. What a job this was, with a large house on the estate for my family, a truck, and good salary. This was wonderful. I worked with my predecessor for a month. Then I moved into the house with my family; and my lurking, trying not to be too obvious, addiction. It must have hitched a ride on the bumper of our car as we drove away from our home in town.

Just like a petri dish is ideal for growing bacteria, this new job, and its setting were ideal for my addiction to fully surface and flourish. It went from occasionally having a few drinks, to eventually driving around in my work truck all day long drunk. I did a fair job of disguising and covering up for a while but eventually everyone recognizes the "elephant in the living room."

Those were painful years for me. Leah, my second daughter was also born during this period. I can remember trying to stay sober and there would be a huge inner battle that had an emotional component, as well as a physical one.

The emotional component was fueled by my baggage. I was a perfectionist and I experienced a great deal of frustration at work. I was unable to keep the estate at the level I thought it should be kept. I did the job equal to my predecessor, maybe better. The owners were satisfied with my performance (before my drinking got bad), but I was not. This frustration, and lack of fulfillment, began to overheat my emotional boiler.

The physical component was literally like having a gorilla on my back. This was not DTs (delirium tremens: alcohol withdrawal), that would come later. The best way to describe it was that I would actually physically feel as though a large man, or gorilla, was behind me, resting with his full weight on my shoulders and head. Picture his arms draped over both my shoulders dangling down onto my chest and his chin resting on my forehead. There was actual pressure on my forehead. I don't know that I've ever heard anyone else describe it this way, but this was my experience. Maybe that's the origin of the phrase, "having a monkey on your back."

In this struggle I would eventually, and inevitably, give in. I began to see it as a losing battle and, rather than fight, and eventually buckle under the force, I would save myself unnecessary grief and just give in. I remember the relief when I would take that first pull from the bottle; at that point all was well with the world and Rob!

Things got worse and worse. I lost my job but, more importantly, the fabric of my marriage was being destroyed. I did not recognize the severity of the damage being done to my family. Addiction blinds its target; it would be twenty years down the road before I would have a clue as to the harm done to those around me. I honestly thought my wife was overreacting.

I was going to church and trying to live the way I knew God wanted me to, but when it came to using, I was powerless. I felt so weak, so much the failure, in every facet of my life, a failure. There was also unbelievable guilt and remorse. All these things added fuel to the fire, and grease to the soles of my feet. I was speeding downhill and there seemed to be nothing that could slow this runaway train, much less stop it. My view, as I write this now, is one of retrospect, it was not so clear to me then.

I'm sure it was sad, and frustrating, for family and friends to watch my life deteriorate before their eyes and watch me seemingly doing little about it. Maybe a good analogy here would be someone caught in a riptide and being pulled out to sea. In my surfing days, before drugs, I was caught in a powerful riptide. I truly feared for my life, and it was probably the hand of God that saved me. This riptide of addiction is not easily escaped either. In an oceanic riptide the way to break free is to swim parallel to the shore until you break free of its pull; you do not face it head-on. If you don't know this, you will most likely lose the battle. I, like the swimmer facing the current head-on, was no match for its power and was losing ground and sight of the shoreline.

The disadvantage those around me had was that they saw only the normal-looking surface of the sea, the current that had me was just below, invisible to the untrained eye. Interestingly, it would be that same hand of God that saved me from the riptide, off the coast of Morro Bay, that would rescue me from my addiction many years later.

II

The Shore is Harder to See

———

After losing my job we needed to move because our home was tied to my employment on the estate. Our parents, both mine and Lene's, helped us purchase a home. As great as it was to have our own home, the current of my addiction continued to pull me further out to sea.

My drinking, and all that came with it, killed my relationship with my wife. Honesty and trust were long things of the past. Lene told me that I had deserted her. I could not understand that at the time. I do now. My judgment, and my perception of the way things were, was so far from the truth, that I believed she was being unreasonable.

One day, I came home from work, drunk as usual, but this time something was different. When I came in, Lene greeted me pleasantly, said nothing about my drinking, and we had an uneventful dinner and evening. This was good, but too good. This happened several days in a row. Had she finally seen the light? Was she now OK with my drinking? Had she finally recognized her exaggerated response to my generally well-behaved drinking? She had started attending some meetings; they called them "Alanon" or something. I was all for these meetings; whatever was going on there must be good. They were probably teaching her drinking wasn't so bad, and to get off my back. Finally the voice of reason! This new utopia was short lived.

A week or two later, I came home drinking as usual, expecting to meet my newly enlightened wife, and instead was met with a restraining order, a three-day notice to vacate, and a support order. The rug had just been ripped out from under me. In one fell swoop I lost my family, my home, and two-thirds of my livelihood. This was a devastating and punishing blow. I can say now, Lene did the right thing, the needful thing, for herself, our two daughters, and for me. She along with family, friends, and church family had done everything they could; they would not be sucked out to sea with me. Addiction, if you let it, will seriously harm all those around the addict. Just as the destructive forces of flying shrapnel reach far beyond the detonation site of an exploding boom, so is the destructive reach of addiction. At some point there must be a separation from the addict for the good of ALL.

It is my experience, and observation, in my recovery, and the recovery of others whose process I have been a part of, that pain is what motivates change. No addict is served by being shielded from the painful results of their addiction. For years, I hated Lene for what she had done, but I have since become thankful. Lene helped me, saved herself, and most importantly, rescued Angela and Leah, and took on the difficult task of raising our daughters alone with no help from me. For this, I will forever be grateful.

12

Last Call

————

With the loss of my home and family, I entered into a level of emotional pain that was greater than anything I had previously experienced. This was, at this point, a separation, not yet a divorce. I was being given yet another opportunity to turn things around.

Along with this separation came, not only the loss of family, friends, and home, but a sense of place and identity. Where do I fit now? Lene got the family, friends, and home. I was seen, and probably rightly so, as the problem, and the source of all this madness. So then, who am I now? Am I a husband now? How can I be a father in this setting? Then there is the element of rejection, and the pain, and shame, of that. I felt unwanted and discarded, like an old pair of worn-out underwear. I was back to ground zero in the insecurity and self-worth departments. I had experienced rejection in the past, but this cut deeper than anything I had ever known. I don't know if bringing this on myself added to the pain. I know that I, very much, felt mistreated. The very nature of separation and divorce makes it a painful process. I lashed out in response to my own pain and sense of helplessness.

In marriage, there is a knitting together of two souls and they truly do become one, even in the midst of dysfunction. When the two separate there is no clean break, but there is a tearing, with the two halves each leaving and taking fragments of the other with them. Imagine if you will a skin graft. Two pieces of skin are brought together, and grow together to become one, it is now not possible to separate the two cleanly. Separation is messy at best and then you still have raw exposed flesh to deal with. I felt raw, I felt fragmented. Where's my medication? The bottle was what I knew.

My recollection of things from this point on is sketchy at best. I had a period of sobriety while in residence at New House, a sober living program for men in Santa Barbara. I tried, but I had no idea what it would eventually take to get right. In that period of sobriety I didn't know what my wife wanted to see in order to reconcile. Now, being many years sober, I understand what she needed to see. Genuine recovery speaks for itself, it is hard to quantify, but easily recognized. It encompasses much more than physical sobriety; that is but the beginning point. Back then I didn't get it, I couldn't have. What was so clear to Lene still escaped me.

In an effort to repair our marriage we met regularly with our pastor and his wife. I was not drinking at this time, but I was smoking a lot of pot. I smoked on the way to the counseling sessions. This was during my second stay at New House sober living. I also smoked pot in my truck in front of my daughters during visits. I thought they were too young to understand what was going on. They told their mom I smoked sour cigarettes, Lene got it. Needless to say the counseling ended.

As time went on things got worse. I was becoming more distant from my family and my using escalated. My drinking got worse and cocaine had come into the picture. One night I decided to pay a visit to my old home and was jailed for violating a restraining order. No one in the family would bail me out. My employers found out where I was, posted bail, and picked me up at the jail. I worked at the "County Bowl," a 4,500-seat outdoor amphitheater, where we, at that time, hosted rock concerts and other events. I was jailed just prior to a big show and was needed. They weren't aware of how bad things were in my personal life, and my behavior hadn't raised any red flags in that environment.

With all the stabilizing forces in my life now gone, family, friends, and church, I truly felt alone and adrift. I was no longer a husband, and how much of a father was I really? Who was I, and where did I fit now? After failing in marriage and being utterly rejected, I again felt like that insecure schoolboy I had once been. The difference being, I was now in my late twenties. In the years that followed, I struggled to find my place as well as my way; never feeling comfortable in polite society, always seeking the companionship of others like myself. Regardless of where I was or who I was with, I always felt very alone. The great losses I had experienced created an inner sense of defeat that colored the lenses I viewed all of life through. I learned to settle for what I could get. There is a heartache and despair that comes from repeated failure. I have often said, "I got my master's in failure and my doctorate in defeat."

The "normie," or nonaddicted, looks on and thinks, "You did this to yourself, just stop." That is a little like saying to the swimmer caught up in a riptide, "You did this to yourself, just get out." It is not that simple, there is less free will at this point than there would appear to be.

During my stays at New House, in Santa Barbara, I met and became close with several veteran alcoholics. I gravitated to the "old-timers," the young ones under forty, were, for lack of a better term, too unsettled. For many years, these men had traveled the road I had only just begun to travel. Externally we were different, but we were the same on the inside; our hopes and dreams, the painful losses and crushing defeats, and the same hopes of escaping an entire life ruled and governed by our addictions. I am able to see now that I experienced and received the companionship and acceptance from Bob and Chet that I didn't get from my dad. I have often said, and still hold it to be true today, "The neatest people I have known have been those who have experienced and survived the pain of addiction."

For the most part, chemically dependent folk enter the gates of addiction as a result of their preexisting woundedness, experienced in family and community. Add to that, the effects of addiction, and over time you have a person left with very little pretense. An ongoing struggle I have is the apparent posturing in polite society. There is no place this bothers me more than in the church. As one who has served as a pastor in the church (since getting sober), I believe church folk could learn much from those in recovery. By necessity, recovering people have had to take a hard and honest look at themselves, own their junk, and ask God to help them clean it up. As a result of this process they have been able to ask God for help, accept and embrace who they are, and live freely before God and the people around them. We all have "stuff," but sadly not all realize it.

13

It's Not What, But Why

I t must have been becoming quite clear to Lene by now that I was locked on a course of self-destruction, and there would be little hope of change. The final step would need to be taken. I was in rehab again, when I was served with divorce papers. This was a shock, but not a surprise, if that makes any sense. My addiction prevented me from having a true and accurate grasp of my situation. The severity and finality of this step was an emotional blow the likes of which I had never experienced. I remember being on my knees bent over my bed in such emotional pain that my cries carried no sound.

I was not the victim here, that would have made it easier. I had put myself in this position. I was losing my precious girls, and my wife wanted nothing to do with me. I was experiencing great loss and rejection, and the pain was horrible. Adding to that was the knowledge, that I alone bore the responsibility.

Being an addict is like being in a maze, wanting out, searching possible pathways of escape, but finding only the passageways leading deeper and deeper into the labyrinth of addiction. There is a widely held misconception that "addicts are just weak willed." Nothing could be further from the truth. Look at a long-term addict and you will see a strong-willed, determined individual, willing to take risks, willing to do whatever it takes to accomplish his or her task, and to do this with declining health, the risk of imprisonment, and the opposition of society and family. This is no wimp.

Few nonaddicts are able to grasp the monumental struggle of the addicted. The perspective of an onlooker is much different for two reasons: one, the onlooker's senses are not clouded, but clear; and two, the onlooker's perspective is not limited to that of the complex confines of a bewildering prison. No addict can escape addiction under his or her own power, but to the free onlooker, the solution appears to be simple enough—just stop, and walk away! If it were truly that simple there would be very few addicts.

Now I had lost my family, and as they slipped away so did what little footing I had. This began a slow but steady slide further into the pit. As my using increased so did my distain for my ex-wife. My world began to shrink. It consisted of a long string of meaningless jobs, the companionship of others like me, and a never-ending succession of rehab attempts. From about 1980 to February 6, 1997 it was all the same, like the movie, *Groundhog Day*. In the movie, the lead character, played by Bill Murray, is stranded in Punxsutawney, Pennsylvania, where he is, by way of an alternate reality, subjected to repeating the same day over and over again. It is here, in an endless succession of Groundhog Days, that he eventually comes to the end of himself and institutes core changes in the way he addresses life. Unlike the movie, my life was more tragedy than comedy, and as the years, rather than days, wore on, things got uglier.

I was on my own, no one caring now if I stayed clean or not, no one looking over my shoulder. If I needed to medicate myself before, I certainly needed it all the more now.

I learned to paint houses and managed to get by. At some point I came back to Visalia for two weeks to paint my parents' home, eight weeks and four houses later, I decided to move back to Visalia. I returned to Santa Barbara, emptied out the bedroom

I was renting, loaded all my worldly possessions into my 1956 Chevy pickup, and moved home, in with my parents. Boy, if that isn't the self-esteem builder every divorced young man needs!

At this point I was smoking a lot of weed. Some months earlier, (while still living in Santa Barbara), I had gone through Schick Shadel Hospital. It was at that point I ended a heroin run and was treated for my alcoholism.

Initially I was intrigued by their treatment approach, they used sodium pentathol (truth serum), and you got to drink. In fact you were required to drink. How this helped, I didn't care, it sounded like my kind of rehab.

I was admitted, and the first phase was a closely monitored medical detox. The next step was the first in a series of five sodium pentathol treatments that would alternate every other day, leapfrogging the aversion therapy treatments, for a total of ten treatments. The sodium pentathol did a couple of things: first and very importantly, it provided an excellent state of rest down to the cellular level; and second, the staff was able to determine the effectiveness of the aversion therapy as treatment progressed.

The aversion therapy, or Duffy treatments, as they were referred to were tough. The name came from a patient who hung a sign that read "Duffy's Tavern" on the door of the treatment room. The room and treatments have affectionately carried the name ever since. ("Duffy's Tavern" was the name and setting of a radio show popular from 1940 through the early 1950's as well as a film released in 1945.) The Duffy room was probably six feet by eight feet in size and decorated with all the glitz of a fine drinking establishment. There was a large mirror that reflected all the beauty and splendor of the mirrored bottles, lights, and illuminated signage that filled the room. There was one object that seemed oddly out of place and that was a straight-backed armchair made of wood and steel—this was in place of a comfortable padded bar stool. Oh, one other component of that straight-backed chair was a large stainless steel basin on a swivel arm that closed you in when you sat down, a little like the safety bar on a carnival ride. The basin should have been a big red flag, but its ominous appearance was overshadowed by the glamour of the enticing bottles and the thoughts and excitement of knocking back a few.

Before I go further, let me explain the premise of this treatment. Aversion therapy is based on the concept of conditioned response. Behavior modification is achieved for a drinker when the positive feelings associated with alcohol are replaced in the psyche of the drinker with negative ones. When you take a drink you feel good. This link overrides the desire to quit, no matter how pressing and desperate the need to stop may be. Behavior modification addresses this by linking negative and unpleasant responses when a drink is taken. Very simply put, DRINK=GOOD is changed to DRINK=BAD.

Now, back to the Duffy room. It is here that you are met by a member of the top-notch nursing staff. Before sitting down you are given an injection. As I remember it, this was a multidrug cocktail, with each drug having a unique function. The combined effect of this was that the alcohol in the drinks in which you were about to indulge would never be absorbed, and their presence would make you so violently ill that they very shortly filled that stainless steel basin in front of you. You enter the room thinking you will get to drink, and leave the room having been required to drink. In the first treatment you are served three drinks and that number is substantially increased with each successive treatment. The Duffy room is a place you quickly come to dread. When you leave there it's not over. You are then taken to a quiet room where you crawl into bed. It is here you spend several hours feeling your pain. About the time things begin to subside a lovely member of the nursing staff brings you a shot glass of something that rekindles that fading agony. Awhile later you reenter the land of the living, relieved and grateful it's over.

This treatment, as difficult as it was, made sense to me. Leaving the facility, and following through with all the recommended aftercare, I had every confidence in the world that I had now been "fixed."

There were some things that were definitely true: one, I had no desire whatsoever to drink, and two, nothing at the core of my being had changed. As time went on it became evident the internal struggles were still present, and continued to tear at me, in spite of the counseling and aftercare. So what do I do now? I couldn't drink now, even if I wanted to—that had been ruined—and in that regard the treatment had been a success. I didn't want to use, I wanted sobriety, but something had to be done to quiet that oh-so-familiar gorilla that was still with me. Pot was a small thing, it certainly wasn't harmful like heroin or meth. Maybe that would appease that agitated gorilla, and besides, I had always been able to control weed.

I was soon smoking like I drank, all day long. The difference being I couldn't get hammered on weed like I could with the bottle or heroin.

A short time after moving back to Visalia I began using cocaine and meth, I could now drop the pot. With the coke and meth I needed to start drinking again, they work well together; the problem was, I couldn't. Schick had destroyed my ability to drink with ease or pleasure. So I was now on a mission, I had purpose, I had a goal, I would reclaim my ability to drink and enjoy it. This was no easy task. It seemed to take about a week of sipping beer, gradually more and more, until I could drink enough to get good and drunk. I was home; a life with no booze was not for me.

I didn't see it then, but I did years later. The problem was not the behavior, but what was on the inside, making the behavior necessary.

14

Go Directly Home, Do Not Pass Go, Do Not Collect $200

I was back at square one, single, living at home with my parents, and trying to hide my drug use. Things were back as they were before I left home. The only difference being I had more wreckage under my belt and I was now about thirty years old. I was a failure, and very much felt like one. Because of my internal pain, drugs and alcohol were more essential now than ever before.

Years earlier I had began using as a means of coping with my feelings of insecurity and inadequacy, but the net affect was I became more insecure and experienced a greater sense of inadequacy. Using crippled my ability to successfully navigate life and, in fact, invited destructive forces into my world. Drug use at any level is not benign.

I had now been away from Visalia for ten years. Years earlier I had left to go to rehab, then married, and moved to Santa Barbara. I was back now and much had changed. People were scattered; some were in prison, a few were dead, and others, who knew. I gradually began finding my way around. Visalia had grown and much had changed. I slowly began to connect and find a few old faces, many of which were still doing what we were doing years earlier. We were older now and locked into a way of life.

Coming back was bittersweet. Santa Barbara had increasingly become an ill-fitting and painful place for me to be. Although I was raised here, coming back to Visalia was a bit of a culture shock. Santa Barbara is a place of extreme beauty with much to do and very laid back. Visalia, on the other hand, was not so laid back, and culturally a few years behind. I have always been a better cultural fit to Visalia than Santa Barbara. What I'm referring to is world view and approach to life. I am very much a small-town conservative in my thinking. Believe it or not, even as an addict I was a law-and-order guy and always understood the risks I took. It generally took a felony, or at least a misdemeanor or two per day, to maintain my habit.

So, where and how do I fit now? Feeling like I fit in had always been a difficult thing for me, and now, back home, divorced, and living with my parents, it was no easier. The pain and rejection of losing my family had left me with not a leg to stand on when it came to any kind of confidence, or self-worth needed to venture out relationally. Earlier in life drugs had helped me socially, but they were no longer a help, they had actually had a crippling effect. I had long since come to a place where I could not venture out without being under the influence. Drugs had become the central focus of my existence and I had no life apart from them.

There is another great limitation that I experienced, and that was a lack of age-appropriate emotional maturity. Living in the bottle, or the bag, circumvents normal emotional development and this emotional dwarfism has the same effect in the emotional and social arenas that physical dwarfism has in the physical. It is very difficult to navigate life when everything and everyone is bigger than you are. This is an acquired developmental barrier and one of the many complex components of the prison of addiction. Emotionally I was still seventeen or eighteen years old, and an emotional dwarf. Consequently I gravitated to others like myself.

I was back home now just as devoid of purpose and focus as I had been years before. Drugs and the major life defeat of a divorce had depleted me of any ambition, even of having my own place. My share of the profit from the sale of our home was now gone, or about gone, and I was starting down the road of the deadbeat dad. I believe in a divorce both parties are hurt and both feel that they have been mistreated, I certainly did. I felt I had been screwed, that I had been discarded like a bit of rubbish and now, "you want me to pay too." My position was simple, I will do what I can and if that isn't good enough, put me in jail. I was taken to court three times, and I was ready to go to jail, but it never came to that. This was not about wanting to neglect my daughters, but it was about drawing a line in the sand and saying, enough is enough. I was mad as hell and wasn't going to take it anymore. There was so much anger and bitterness in me that I determined I would destroy what few assets I had left rather than let anything more be taken from me and given to my ex-wife.

One of the freedoms I now enjoy is the freedom from the hate that once consumed me. There came a time (fifteen years later) when God helped me to do what I could not do on my own, and that was to forgive. Just as importantly, He enabled me to see my part and to ask for forgiveness, which was graciously and willingly given.

Nothing in life is static, and this is very evident in addiction. My addiction was consuming more and more of me. In the 1958 science fiction thriller *The Blob* starring Steve McQueen, a life form from outer space originally started out quite small but grew exponentially with each new victim it consumed. As the Blob grew it became a greater and more menacing threat. Addiction, like the Blob, has an Achilles' heel. For the blob it was cold, for the addict it is surrender to a power greater than addiction.

Even though I had lost so much, as a direct result of an ever increasing and consuming addiction, I was determined to make this work. I was going to continue to use without further loss. I no longer had any reason not to use, and every reason to continue. The feelings of great loss, rejection, and failure were like a team of three wild stallions dragging me further into the abyss of addiction. The pain of an addict, though much of it, at this point, is self-generated, continues to drive the addict further into a place of isolation and desperation and deeper into the jaws of the beast.

There is a slow and insidious, less-than-obvious, process that runs parallel to the course of addiction. Just as a mason works parallel to a wall adding brick and block to thicken and raise it, so does this process add to the stature of the walls that imprison the addicted. The building blocks of these walls are the losses, disappointments, and failed attempts at sobriety, that clutter an addict's life. And the mortar for these building blocks is the constant and ever-present, and oftentimes undiscerned, drone of emotional pain generated by a conflicted soul. Regardless of how it may appear to the onlooker, the addict pays a huge price internally. These things combined are adding thickness and height to the walls that imprison the addict.

There is still another element of addiction that is best illustrated by a tragic event that took place during the years of World War II. There is a story told of an experiment done in a Nazi concentration camp. The prisoners were normally assigned jobs such as road building and repair, and the laying and repairing of railway lines, all being hard manual labor. The experiment was to see the response of the prisoners to a never-ending series of meaningless tasks. These jobs would have the same physical demands as their regular duties; the only difference being that it would be apparent to the prisoners the tasks had no real purpose or value.

The experiment began. A group of prisoners were told to move a very large mound of dirt and rubble to another location in the compound. They did so with shovels, buckets, and wheelbarrows. After completing the task they were ordered to move the same mound back to where it had originally been. This process was repeated over and over again. This began to do to the men what near starvation and grueling, backbreaking labor could not. As this went on, the prisoners began reaching their breaking point. These men began to commit suicide by running into the electrified barrier wire; they would run as if attempting an escape so the guards would shoot them or take other actions that would result in their deaths.

One of the many observations that were made was this: you can starve, beat, and brutalize people, and they can go on, but rob people of hope and they will lose all desire and will to live.

The experiment I have just described to you is a very real parallel to the second phase of my addiction. Phase I was the birth, growth, and development of my addiction. Phase II comprised the consuming and crippling years. It is this second phase that I am just beginning at this point in my story and it will last about fifteen years.

15

The Press Begins

Years ago there was a luggage commercial and the purpose of the ad was to illustrate the strength and durability of the product. In this ad a piece of luggage was placed in a cage with a live gorilla. This suitcase was jumped on, thrown against the bars, and terribly mistreated; in spite of the rough treatment, it suffered no damage. In the case of addiction, the addict that is caged in with the gorilla of addiction does not fare as well.

I stated earlier that my intention was to continue using, but to do so and suffer no further loss or harm. This was the voice of denial and the thinking of the yet naive. This is a line of thinking prevalent in the mind of the addicted. I was fooled into thinking this gorilla in my life was a cute chimpanzee I could train and control. I had yet to learn what it was like to be caged in and at the mercy and whim of my addiction. Just as when a gorilla begins to slam you around and you have no say as to how, when, or if, it will end, so I would be at the mercy of my addiction.

Many of the old demons I had escaped years earlier when I had left for Los Angeles were now back, attracted like vultures are to an injured beast bleeding in the field. These demons filled out the ranks of those who accompanied me back home.

As I settled in, back where it all started, I slowly got reconnected and began to familiarize myself with the changed terrain of Visalia. In many ways I was starting from scratch. People had scattered and the old haunts were gone, it had been eleven years. I continued using coke and meth, and after a bit of work, was able to discard the weed and pick up the bottle again. I must commend Schick; they did a good job of removing my ability to drink. It took a concerted effort, but I was able to reverse the aversion to drink, and in a short time could drink as I did before. What you have just read is a clear demonstration of addicted thought.

My addiction had two parts. One, I had become dependent physically and emotionally. Physically I needed to use to function, and emotionally, not using would be like trying to get around on one leg, it could be done, but with great difficulty. Drugs also helped me avoid the pain that had become my constant companion, the pain of a failed marriage, the loss of my daughters, and the pain that comes along with being rejected and discarded. These things had begun to define me. I saw myself as a giant zero, a nothing of the first order. I didn't even have a circle of friends. I had a single purpose, that was to stay loaded, and my dealings with people were limited to what was necessary to accomplish that purpose. It was drugs that gave me my emotional fix. It was people, on the other hand, that had always been a source and avenue by which pain had come. As time went on I would ride the rails of the loner more and more. I would interact but always kept people at arm's length; closeness creates vulnerability. All was well in the world, and with Rob, when I had a full bottle and a few bags of dope. And as time went on, add a gun to that.

An incident that took place around this time sticks in my mind and reminds me how I felt about myself. I was sick and had some familiar symptoms so I went to my doctor and he ordered some blood work. I still remember how I felt when I went to have the blood drawn. I sat down with the lab tech, a nice young gal. I felt so dirty, so untouchable. I remember being apologetic that she had to touch me. She was very nice and I know now she had no idea what was going on with me. I was so lonely, yet felt so untouchable, so in need of closeness, yet afraid to let anyone near, so ashamed of who, and what, I had become. The tests confirmed it was hepatitis again.

My insides were much more raggedy than my outside. The greatest devastation in my life was internal. The outer façade never betrayed the whole truth. I worked hard and became skilled at image management. That was a necessary skill to stay out of trouble with the law, and also needed in the arena of creative financing *(lying, manipulating, and stealing)* of my habit.

People are like icebergs; what you see is only a small fraction of what is really there.

16

Enter the Mother of All Addictions

A central principle with addiction is, "what once satisfied, no longer does." It is this principle at work that demands the addict go deeper. You will find this true with any addiction, whether it be drugs, alcohol, sex, food, anger, and so on. My addiction had an insatiable appetite and the coke and booze were no longer enough, so I turned to an old friend, heroin. Heroin had been my drug of choice in my earlier years but, while married and living in Santa Barbara, alcohol and cocaine were a better fit. For the sake of clarity the cocaine came after my marriage ended.

When you change drugs you change the circles you run in. This means the other addicts you run with change (birds of a feather), and the people you do business with also change. Each drug has a world of its own. In Visalia, as is true throughout the west and southwest, the Mexicans own the heroin trade. My preference was to do business with border-brothers, these were Mexican nationals. With these men it was business, they had no habit to feed, which will dramatically change the way you do business. We got along well and I preferred them over whites or Mexican Americans. In spite of an occasional language barrier I was accepted and treated better by the border-brothers than by the others, and I knew my purchases would always be what I paid for. I was never cheated.

I was living a double life, unlike most of the people I did business with or ran with. This in itself makes life difficult and creates an inner conflict. Anytime people are not, or cannot, be honest about who they are, or what they do, a destructive inner force is created. With my parents, with whom I was living, and eventually my second wife, my addiction eventually became like the elephant in the living room; everyone knew it was there but we didn't talk much about it. Even so, I tried to live life with them like a normie (nonaddict). That worked about as well as trying to hold a beach ball under the water at the beach, no matter how valiant the effort, it's going to pop up to the surface.

There was an intense drive to use, and a fear of withdrawal that accompanied my heroin addiction, and these grew as my addiction grew. The drive to use was by no means new to me, but heroin took this drive and gave it a turbo-boost. There was a demand to be fed and that required a constant flow of cash. The income generated by legitimate means such as house paint-ing, although paying well, did not always go far enough or come in adequately to meet my daily needs. When I did get a large sum of money I would use more, unable to ration my dope to cover a given period. This cash flow problem, and the eventual debilitating effect using had on my ability to work, led me more and more into crime as a funding source.

I once went on a cruise with my parents to celebrate their fiftieth wedding anniversary. It was Mom and Dad, my two sisters and their husbands, and me and my second wife and my heroin habit. I had promised my wife I would kick it and be clean by the time we went on the cruise; I had not kicked and was not clean. I planned and stocked up enough dope to last the four days, it was gone in less than two. What do you do on a ship in the Pacific, miles off shore? You go to the ship's doctor. I was able to get a refill on a codeine prescription I had, now I was set. A day and half after that, I was back, needing a refill on a prescription that should have lasted a minimum of a week. I played it off like I misunderstood the dosing instructions, and I got another refill. This heroin addiction clearly had me by the shorts. That was the demand to feed the addiction.

The second driving force of heroin addiction is the physical withdrawal you experience when your system begins to hit empty. This is the enforcer of the addiction. It can be compared to the guy who pays you a visit when you are behind on your weekly "strokes" to the neighborhood loan shark. He leaves you with the pain of crushed ribs and broken kneecaps to coerce you to fall back in line and pay up. It was the fear of this enforcer that I went to sleep with and woke to each morning. It was his nudging that drove me out of bed each day to pursue my wake-up fix.

I have a very vivid experience etched in my memory and it has as much to do with how I felt emotionally as how and what I was doing physically. It was a cold morning, but I was very cold, hunched over the steering wheel of my '68 Volkswagen van with my beanie pulled down over my ears. I was driving down Goshen Avenue along with the other early morning commuters. My bones ached, my bowels were churning, and my goal was to score and get a needle in my arm before I messed my pants. I remember in the midst of that drive looking at the regular folks sipping their coffee on their way to work, and seeing the difference between us. I wondered if I could ever be like them and live a normal life.

When I remember those years, there are no thoughts of the "good ole days." What comes back to me so vividly is the pain, the feelings that accompany slavery, and over time, the loss of hope. It was the accumulation of this internal pain that eventually brought me to that place of **surrender.**

It has been my observation that internal forces draw a person into addiction, internal forces fuel that addiction, and internal forces drive the exodus from addiction.

17

The Wheels Begin to Wobble

I had entered the last decade of my using career. These last years were the roughest.

A few years ago I watched a televised police chase that I believe took place in Los Angeles, or maybe Miami. As it went on I watched in amazement at the lengths this driver went to escape the clutches of the police.

The initial pursuit began after the driver failed to yield to police after a relatively minor traffic violation. After repeated attempts by authorities to stop him, "stop sticks" were deployed. As the driver passed over the sticks his tires were punctured and began to deflate, slowing the vehicle and making it difficult to control. To my amazement the driver continued and as he did, the tires, now flat, began to fly apart and soon the car was traveling on bare rims. By now the engine was smoking terribly and the driver's vision was obscured by the billowing smoke coming from under the hood and engulfing the passenger compartment. The road was now being littered by miscellaneous parts falling from the vehicle as this unbelievable pursuit continued to exact its toll.

Have you ever wondered, as I have, "What are these people thinking?" The chase finally ended when the car slid off the road into a ditch.

I have recognized two components in the thinking of the "runners" that have been caught and questioned, and they are these: fear and irrational thought.

My using career very much parallels this chase. I kept going even after the tires separated and flew off. I also collided with, and injured, many innocent bystanders along the way. I too was driven by fear and irrational thought, the fear and irrational thought of my addiction.

The last ten years of my addiction were tough. This period was littered with many, many attempts to "get right." My using was sucking me dry, sucking every bit of life and hope out of me. Have you ever eaten a piece of chicken to the point where you are sucking on the bones? It was to that extent that my addiction was devouring me. I would go until I could go no further, and then, out of desperation, enter a program, hoping for change. Each stop along the way was an opportunity, and I was slowly, and incrementally, making my way to the place of surrender, surrender without reservations.

I have come to so clearly understand that surrender is the one **nonnegotiable** ingredient in the foundation on which recovery is built. The surrender I'm speaking of is embodied in the first three steps of the "12 steps." Simply put, "I can't, God can, and I'll let Him." Surrender is not giving up to being whipped by your addiction, although that is part of it, but surrender is giving full reign to the only One who can restore you, and that one is God, God Himself.

I have tried treatment approaches devised by the best and brightest minds and presented by well-intentioned people and the results were marginal at best. The best tools and approaches are lacking when God is not at the center of your efforts. It was only after surrendering to God that I began to experience genuine internal change. Recovery must be from the inside out. The years since that day, February 6, 1997, have been phenomenal to say the least; they have been more than I could have ever dreamed possible. Every facet of my life has been touched and continues to improve. I have found recovery to be a wonderful ongoing process.

18

The Wheels Fall Off

The end for me was the last year and a half of my addiction.

Just prior to this period I was in the PAAR Center in Porterville, it was my third tour. After the initial ninety-day period I stayed and became house manager. I got room and board and received a modest stipend. I eventually assumed the role of program coordinator. I loved my work and was good at it. I taught classes, led groups, counseled, and took care of the administrative paperwork. I was young in recovery for much of what I was doing, but it worked, and by all accounts I was doing a good job.

It was during this period that I lost my dad to a fatal heart attack. He had his first attack in 1975, and over the next nineteen years the medical community was able to do much to prolong Dad's life with surgeries and an implanted electrical device. Dad did his part by changing his diet, giving up tobacco, and staying active. Giving up smoking for him was no small thing; he had been a smoker since the age of eight.

Staying active was a natural thing for Dad. He was regularly building or fixing something, or going on an errand to find a part or tool. Dad also instituted regular walks as a part of his regimen. Mom, a retired nurse and loving wife, was concerned that something might happen to Dad during one of these walks and he would be unable to get help. This was before the era of small portable cell phones. His response was typical "Dad." He numbered each of the different routes he took, then drove each one to determine the exact distance, then walked each one to determine walking time. Then prior to leaving the house for his walk he would give Mom the number of the route he was taking. Dad's thinking was that if he was not back within the allotted time, Mom would know where to find his body. This did not set her at ease. Mom had tried walking with Dad, but she, having shorter legs, made the pace of little therapeutic value for Dad.

In our home the subject of death was not a morbid topic, it was not unusual to hear the phrase, "When you die can I have such and such?" Mom and Dad were secure in where they would spend eternity because of their relationship with God. I, on the other hand, was not, but death would have been a welcome relief from the madness that was an ever-present part of my existence. I have, over the course of my addiction, made a few suicide attempts. In all actuality, I believe only one was serious; the others were more like veiled cries for help.

Dad was not one to talk much about feelings—yours or his. That was difficult for him. Growing up, I understood he loved me, and throughout my life I always greeted Dad, and said good-bye, with a kiss. I was also taught to greet elder family members, such as grandparents and great-aunts and uncles in this way as a sign of affection and respect. This mirrored Dad's relationship with his father. In the midst of this genuine affection, I always sought and searched for his approval, never feeling I got it. The day I was called at work, and then rushed to the intensive care unit to be with Dad, was the first time in my life I felt needed and accepted by him. As I walked in I saw the look I had longed for all my life; he needed me, and he was relieved and glad to see me. Over those three days we said our good-byes, we both understood this was the end, our good-byes were said without words. It was here that Mom put Dad's ring on my finger.

Dad was a man of great integrity, moral fiber, and a caring heart. His demeanor was that of a hard and unapproachable man, very unlike who he truly was. I am told, and have observed myself, that I am very much like my father. I consider it an honor to be the son of Robert Flammang Sr.

I was still married to my second wife, but saw the marriage as a relationship I could no longer continue to live with. I waited until I had been clean a year before I made the decision to divorce. The relationship was such that I was unwilling to live that way any longer. Being actively addicted most of our marriage, I had become the convenient scapegoat at whose feet all ills and wrongs were laid. Being strung out, I put up with this to keep peace, and over time actually began to believe it. When I got clean, my thinking slowly began to clear. I was slowly no longer being driven by guilt. I was changing; no longer would I be manipulated, controlled, or shamed. My addiction was complicit in the destruction of the marriage. Patterns were set that were difficult to break once I got clean. I was still being held solely responsible for all things and everyone's happiness.

I asked for a divorce, but was not taken seriously. I have been one to con and hustle people, but I have never played games; I was dead serious. After I filed, I was taken seriously. Nine months later the divorce was final and I was finally living alone.

I was living alone and loving it. I commuted to work from Visalia to Porterville. I was clean, fulfilled in my work, free from a difficult marriage; all was well with the world. I had twenty-three months clean and sober, the longest period ever for me since my addiction started twenty-five years earlier.

19

Out of the Blue

————

My second divorce was nearly final, and when my soon-to-be "ex" moved out, I took time off to resettle my home. All was well and I was on my way to do something in town, I don't remember what. I was thrilled to finally have the divorce process coming to a close and settling into my new life, clean, sober, and single.

What came over me next was a desire to use; there was no struggle, no inner battle, surprisingly, no resistance whatsoever. I was caught completely off guard. It was as if I was a city with no walls, or defenses, and an enemy force just walked in, facing absolutely no opposition, and took over. In a half an hour's time I had acquired a syringe and a bag of dope. After using I was determined not to continue the following day, but I did. I never returned to the Center; it was on! For the next year and a half I would be buried in the pit of addiction. It would be this last stretch of my addiction that would bring me to the place of complete and total surrender.

Years later in a conversation with Mom, she told me she felt something was missing in my recovery, and it was not until she saw the level of surrender I eventually came to that she realized what that "missing something" was. The missing something was "surrender," "God, I want your best in my life, I will not use even if it kills me, I will not be ripped off again; <u>whatever</u> it takes, I will do."

After a year and a half of intense daily heroin (methadone at the end) and alcohol use, I came to the end of myself, much like the prodigal son described in the Bible. Inside I could go no further. I went to Mom and asked for her help. I was admitted to Cedar Vista Hospital in Fresno for detox and treatment. At this point I was drinking two fifths of vodka a day and shooting dope throughout the day. At the end it would take four or five hours of slow and careful drinking in bed each morning to get well enough to go get my first fix of the day. The alcohol was more debilitating than the heroin. The booze was really crippling me up, but the dope perked me up and took the aches and stiffness away, much like the oil did for the Tin Man in *The Wizard of Oz*.

The mornings were hell, I woke to both heroin and alcohol withdrawal. One thing that helped me was being on methadone the last half of this period. All I needed to do was drive to Fresno each day to get my dose, and this was good for twenty-four hours. My condition was such that it made it more and more difficult to pull off a convincing con or hustle. I could no longer pull off the "upstanding citizen" thing.

The drinking was crippling me up such that hygiene suffered. Booze really makes you smell, and on top of that, it became too much of a chore to bathe. It became common for me to go a month between showers.

I was still living in my home on the "family compound," as we call it. The "compound" is an acre with two homes on it, the first is the home I grew up in, and the second was built by my grandmother when she moved from San Pedro to Visalia in 1960. I lived in "Mamo's" (my maternal grandmother) house. I lived there alone after the divorce.

You might wonder how I supported myself. I paid no rent, courtesy of Mom; she also covered my utilities and food. I had a regular monthly income from a scheme I devised, and I stole the balance of what I needed.

Early in my story I mentioned going to score with an old veteran dope fiend. I wanted to be able to do what he did, which was to stay loaded without having to keep a regular job. Well, now I was the "veterano." I was staying loaded without keeping a regular job. I had reached one of my life goals. It was in no way what I had thought it would be; the cost had been immense. As a point of interest, according to the Social Security Administration, my taxable income from 1969 through 1997 was $147,829.00, for a twenty-eight-year period. Gainful employment and addiction do not coexist for long. Addiction is an ever-demanding way of life and will settle for nothing less than all you have and are, mind, body, and soul.

Addiction left me in economic ruin, but that was the least of it. The greatest toll was taken emotionally and spiritually. The physical pain of addiction, even as it worsens over time, is pain that you can get some relief from; the inner private pain becomes increasingly harder and harder to quell. It was this unquenchable fire in me that slowly and steadily ushered me into the place of surrender. At the end, no diversion, no amount or combination of dope and booze could bring relief. What started out twenty-eight years earlier as a wonderful source of relief from my internal pain and insecurities now was the very thing that fueled a raging internal inferno that brought me more pain than it ever relieved. I had truly become only a shell of a man.

Mom had always played a crucial role in my life. It was she who did so much to nurture, encourage, and shape my heart. It has been Mom, over the course of my life, who has been my number one cheerleader. It is she who was key to my survival in the last stretch of my addiction. Mom has prayed for me for years, but as the end neared she took it to a new level.

I had decided at some point, that to account for my obvious physical deterioration, I would tell Mom I had AIDS. Another part of my thinking was that if I had AIDS, she would stay off my back about using, if she suspected I was, and I did not want to go over old ground yet again. I am sure I fooled no one about my using, especially at this stage of my addiction. To complete this ruse, and make it solid, I felt it necessary to convince two other key people in Mom's life, her doctor and her pastor. The need to convince Mom's doctor was obvious, since we both went to the same one. Convincing my doctor was crucial to another element of this con I cannot go into. This took some finesse and was done while permitting no blood work. With Mom's pastor, it seemed a nice touch. (It's the attention to detail that make or break a con.) Both these men played important and supportive roles in Mom's life; one physical, one spiritual; she was close to both of them. Later, when I had been in recovery for a while, it was time to make amends and come clean on this issue; Mom was relieved, Doctor B. was shocked and I believe felt hurt and used, and Pastor Albert was speechless. Albert was himself in recovery, and a skilled, knowledgeable, and experienced counselor. This was the one and only time I ever saw him at a loss for words.

One note on the AIDS issue. Over the years I was tested many times as part of the treatment process in the many programs and treatment centers I entered. I remember a tinge of disappointment each time I received the negative results. Part of me wanted it (my addiction) over, and still another part of me wanted to be cared for until the end. This all, in my mind, was more appealing than the life I had endured.

Viewing yourself as a failure, and non achiever most of your life, you learn to revel in success wherever you find it. This AIDS con was one of my greatest achievements. The results were far reaching, but for reasons I will not go into, I will limit its scope to what I have already stated.

One other achievement that stands out happened while I was in the local hospital. I had been admitted for observation after experiencing chest pains. I agreed to admission on the condition I be given methadone for my addiction. Once settled in my room, a bag of dope I had with me began to burn a hole in my pocket. The problem I faced was that I had left my rig (syringe and spoon) at home, fearing the possibility of it being found if my clothes needed to be cut off should I go into cardiac arrest. There was a syringe in my room, but there was a problem: it had just been deposited in a medical waste receptacle that was locked, tamper proof, and secured to the wall. Necessity and desperation are both mothers of invention. After a great deal of consideration, and trial and error, I managed to trip the locking mechanism, removing it from the wall, and bypass the other protective measures, thus liberating the lone syringe. All this was done with a hair comb and the spine of a magazine. Now, I could, and did, shoot the bag of dope. As I said, my accomplishments have been few!

From the moment I woke up in the morning, to when I passed out sometime in the night, I had a drink in one hand and a well-used syringe nearby. It was common to wake up with a spilled drink and another cigarette burn in my clothing, furniture, or bedding. I once came to, still in my chair, with the foam cushion I was sitting on, burned, or melted completely away. What I saw, when I looked down, were the steel spring supports and the floor. It was only the part of the cushion between my legs. How this could happen without injury to me, or a house fire, I will never know for sure. I do believe that there never being a fatal fire was the direct result of my mother's prayers.

Looking over the years, I see that I have not experienced many of the repercussions my contemporaries did. My legal problems were minimal, with almost no jail time over the years, and never a trip to the penitentiary; unlike many that I knew and ran with.

I want to make one thing clear; I was never more than a junkie and a drunk. I do not want the reader of this story to be misled. There was never anything glamorous about my life, and I was never some "nickel-slick" hustler. I was very average, but I did use very hard.

I was coming to the end of myself. As the cumulative weight of twenty-eight years of drug use bore down on me I was finally coming to my breaking point. The loss of family, friends, opportunity, and all my hopes and dreams for life did not do it, although those losses did contribute significantly to the inner emotional pain that I was now experiencing. When I now think of that part of my life, there are no pleasant memories to revisit; my thoughts go directly to the inner hidden pain that was known only by me. That pain cannot be shared or explained, except with another who has walked this path. This pain, coupled with the loss of hope, can reduce to rubble the very strongest of people.

I had hit many "bottoms" over the years, but this was the basement—like the old Laurel and Hardy feature, or maybe it was the Three Stooges, where they fell through floor after floor of a multistory building and finally ended their descent when they hit the basement floor and, as they did, they were crushed by the tangled wreckage and debris from the floors above. It was at this point I went to Mom and said, "I'm dying, help me." She did, and the first step was to get me to Cedar Vista Hospital in Fresno. It was Dr. B. who made a call that cleared the way for a speedy admission. Medical detox or no, I had no illusions about what I was about to face, but it just didn't matter; I could not go any further.

I was done. I was really done.

20

Taking the Leap

I was done. I could not bear to go any further. I had an old girlfriend who introduced me to the phrase, "You play, you pay." There is a cause and effect connected to all we do in life; good produces good, bad brings bad. The Bible teaches that we reap what we sow, and just like in nature there is a period of time between the sowing and the reaping where there is little indication of the harvest to come. It was harvest time and I was paying dearly. I had sown for decades and the weight of the harvest rolling in was burying me alive.

I was in a prison without walls of stone and steel. My life had come to very much resemble that of Papillion, a man imprisoned by the French in 1931 and sent to the infamous penal colony in French Guiana known as Devil's Island. His behavior and repeated escape attempts eventually landed him in a place in the penal colony so isolated that life and sanity were threatened. It was here that the choice became clear, make a truly life-threatening escape attempt or die under the weight of his imprisonment.

Rather than face a succession of never-ending days and years of pointless painful existence, he devised a plan of escape. He would be free, even if he died in the process. All reason and logic were against his success.

This was the place I found myself. I was on my own Devil's Island and I had come to the place that I was willing to do whatever it took to escape. I was truly willing to do anything.

There was a sense of relief as Mom drove me to Cedar Vista Hospital in Fresno for the second time. I was taking the leap. I was desperate. I was in many ways like Papillion. It had been a series of events, a progression, over time, that had brought me to this place. Just as Papillion leaped from the cliff to the churning surf below to his frail coconut raft, not knowing if he would survive the fall, much less find freedom, so I was taking my leap. Like Papillion, my previous failed attempts to escape to freedom only fueled my resolve.

More accurately, I turned off, or fell off, the expressway, hoping I would make it. Using the term "leap" denotes a sense of intention, purpose, and control, none of which I had. "Fell off," is probably more accurate. It was more a passive giving up, a surrender to whatever would come. There was no fight left in me.

Like Papillion, I too had a long succession of failed escape attempts from my prison of addiction, and like him, with each failed attempt came even harsher conditions and a lessening of hope. My imprisonment was killing me; I had little left to lose.

In the evening of my first day of detox, as the black clouds of opiate and alcohol withdrawal began to swallow me and the crush of physical and emotional pain began to build and press in on me, I came to a point of decision and surrender with God. I sat at the edge of my bed, and at what would become the end of my addiction. With a mountain of failure resting on my shoulders, *I surrendered* to God. I acknowledged my past failures and made no promises for the future other than to do my best. What I meant by that was, I would truly do my best, whatever the cost, to be obedient to what I knew He would have me do. I had little hope of any great success considering my well-earned doctorate in failure. Being physically and emotionally stripped was the help I needed to surrender.

My position with God would be decision by decision, choice by choice, what would He have me do.

In 1970 Janis Joplin recorded, "Me and Bobby McGee," my favorite song of all time. This song embodies my two-and-a-half-decade-long search for freedom, purpose, and a true sense of inner peace.

Freedom's just another word for nothing left to lose,
Nothing don't mean nothing, honey, if it ain't free.

These lines always resonated with me and truly described the place to which I had come.

It was out of this seedbed, "a life in ashes," that a new life would emerge like that of the phoenix of ancient mythology.

I had no illusions, no great plan, and in light of over two decades of failed attempts at sobriety, very low expectations. I also, as a result of my failed efforts, had come to the bedrock, the foundational place on which all elements of recovery must rest, and that is, *I can't, maybe God will help me.* The central issue for me was staying clean and living as God would have me live. I was so beat up and depleted on every level that my view of the future consisted of the present moment. It was in these early days of recovery that I began to understand the concept of "one day at a time."

I had come to recognize that all that I had learned about recovery had little to no value unless I got the God part settled. Understanding the pathology of addiction and the mechanics of recovery was not enough; God had to be the centerpiece in my recovery. At some point my own efforts would inevitably fail and I would end up "back in the spoon" again.

The God part of recovery had always been my Achilles' heel. I was raised Catholic, and so believed in God, but more a god of judgment than one who loved me and wanted a relationship with me. This defined my "God wall." I knew God could help me, but would He? Did I matter? Did He care?

I didn't want to become some Bible-toting, suit-wearing square. But the biggest obstacle was not saying "God help me," it was giving up control and living my life His way. I didn't know Him, so I didn't know if I could trust Him.

With everything I had learned and come to understand about my addiction and the recovery process, it had become very clear to me that God could not be an optional or secondary component in my recovery. If I was ever to taste freedom, real lasting freedom, I would first need to say yes to Him.

Over the years, I had many times, out of desperation, shot questionable dope into my arms—taking this leap with God was even more necessary.

21

The Journey Begins

S itting on the edge of my detox bed, I surrendered, I quit, I was done. This was like a long foot chase from the law and after miles of alleys, fences, and ravines, not being able to go another step. This had been a twenty-eight-year run. My surrender conversation was with God, I asked for and acknowledged my need for His help. At that point something changed, I went from fear and uncertainty to being at peace, and knowing I was going to be OK. It was like God reached in and stilled all the fear and anxiety that moments earlier had consumed me. I still faced the full force of alcohol and heroin withdrawal and the entire physical and emotional trauma that brings, but I knew, that I knew, that I knew, that I was going to be OK, and I was.

This was a medical detox. I was monitored and given medication to ease the process. I was now forty-four years old and the older you get the more severe the process becomes. During the last year of my addiction, my alcoholism had progressed to the place that I needed to drink continually, from wake up to pass out. In this last stretch of my addiction I would lay in bed for two or three hours each morning carefully and slowly drinking beer to alleviate the shakes and the general body pain, all the while being careful not to drink too quickly and by so doing start vomiting, vomiting that would inevitably end in the painful dry heaves. Once I had enough in my system I could start my day. If I happened to be on methadone I would drive to the clinic in Fresno, forty-five miles away; otherwise, I went to the connection and began my regime of shooting dope and drinking until I passed out sometime in the night.

With my addiction at this stage, and at my age, the medical detox was a blessing. It was no cakewalk, but I felt safe.

After an initial detox of five days I was moved to the "Addiction Recovery Center," a twenty-eight-day residential treatment program along the Kings River on the outskirts of Reedley, California. I can still remember the drive and the thick detox cloud that still surrounded me. This was unlike my prior stay the year before, where I was discharged and sent home. Within an hour's time of my arrival home, I was at the connections with a needle back in my arm.

The ARC was crucial for me. It was a safe place for me to get my "sea legs," if you will. It took months for my thinking to begin to unscramble and the subtle tremors in my hands and legs to leave. Detox is never enough. A safe, secure environment with accountability is essential.

It was in this environment that I began the process of resocialization and finding community. For recovery to be successful our "playmates" and "playpens" must change. My world had become very narrow and very dark. That was changing, and it terrified me.

My life had become like a house with heavy drapes covering every window, preventing any light from entering. As the recovery process slowly pulled these weighty window coverings back, I reluctantly emerged from the shadows. I was terrified. I felt exposed and naked. Sobriety was scary.

There was an event that took place, while at the ARC, that helped me in a significant way. One day while in group with Kerrie, our primary therapist, the men were presented with a challenge. We were first asked the familiar and foundational recovery question, "To what lengths are you willing to go for your recovery?" Most of the guys said whatever it takes. I, on the other hand, had been watching Kerrie carefully and knew she was good at penetrating defenses, and so, not wanting to walk into a trap, I did not respond. Then she said, "I want all the men to cut off all their facial hair" (mustaches and beards). Bear in mind a foundational premise in recovery; *be willing to follow the instructions of trusted mentors without understanding the why.* These people act as guides helping us to navigate the unfamiliar and difficult terrain of sobriety. I had come to see that Kerrie was not only skilled, but that I could trust there would be good in this, if I took this step. This was no small matter for me. I had, with very few exceptions, had a mustache all of my adult life. This was a well-groomed brush that extended down to cover my mouth; it was part of who I was.

I knew I didn't have all the answers, and if this in some way would help me, I was in. Without taking any public position in group, I went to my room afterward, and while questioning my sanity, took scissors, then a razor, to my walrus-like mustache. I had surrendered to God and had become truly willing to do any and all things needed to recover, whether I understood and agreed, or not. My best thinking had gotten me to this place, so it was evident, my thinking could not get me out.

There I was, with my brush (mustache) in the sink. I was feeling as awkward, naked, and exposed, as a newborn, freshly removed from the security of the womb, and then thrust naked and cold into a very foreign and scary world. I came to recognize how I used my appearance to project an image, and set a wall of defense in place. The image I projected, or hoped to, was one of an unapproachable tough guy. Clean and sober and bare faced, I felt much like the charlatan wizard in the movie, *The Wizard of Oz,* when Dorothy's dog Toto pulled back the curtain and revealed a very human wizard. The booming-voiced, thunder-and-fire, larger-than-life, image was recognized for what it was, an image. Just like the wizard, my image was a complex survival mechanism. I began to see myself through a different set of glasses. I determined then to put that mask aside, and just be me. I will forever be grateful for the way God used Kerrie to help me see.

At that stage of my sobriety, it was much like coming out of a twenty-eight-year coma and adjusting to the world as I now began to see it, and having to discover who I really was in the process.

As the days turned to weeks, and the weeks to months, the sky slowly became blue again, and I once again noticed the birds singing. I was coming back to life.

In those very early days of recovery, my life was simple. I would eat, shower, shave, brush my teeth, rest, and go to a meeting. These activities took most of the day to accomplish. My capacity for the duties and responsibilities of life slowly increased over the months and years, and now, twelve years later, is very normal for a man my age.

22

Peeking Through the Cobwebs

I was enjoying my newfound freedom from the bag and bottle. I was also enjoying the camaraderie that is shared, especially by those in early recovery. It is probably more accurate to refer to early recovery as "detox." Although it is in the first week or so that the major part of physical detox is accomplished, it is in the following weeks and months to come that the gradual process of emotional sobriety begins to take form, and it is also in this protracted period of time that physical detox runs its course.

I believe one of the mercies of recovery is that we are generally incapable of truly understanding the gravity of our condition. It has been a process over many years of recognizing the effects my addiction had on me physically, mentally, and emotionally.

While I was still at the ARC I had a major bout with depression. It became so severe that "taking a bullet" looked good. I mentioned this to a counselor, and then there came the attempt at subtle probing to determine if I needed to be put on suicide watch. I was familiar with this process so I told them what I needed to, to avoid being put on suicide watch. Eventually it passed and things went from black back to gray. The guilt, shame, and remorse over the life I had led still weighed heavily on me.

You will oftentimes hear of the "pink cloud" (euphoria) in early recovery. Well, the closest I ever got to a pink cloud it was someone else's, and I wanted to slap them right off of it. Getting clean has always been a tough process for me.

I slowly began finding my way around. There were a handful of meetings I felt comfortable in, and it was in these groups that I began to find a sense of community. These were all out-of-town meetings I had started attending while I was in the ARC.

At about five months into my recovery, things began to shift. At the center of my newly found freedom was God, and it was out of my relationship with Him that everything flowed. I was unable to speak as freely about this facet of my recovery in my meetings as I would have liked. This can be a difficult and oftentimes awkward line to walk in traditional recovery groups. My meetings that had been such a good fit were now leaving me wanting. These groups and the great people in them hadn't changed, I had. It was now time for some additional things in my recovery diet. Just as we change types and styles of footwear over time, so do our needs in recovery change as we grow.

Years earlier, I had been introduced to First Step Recovery, a Christ-centered 12 step group. This was a group that happened to meet at the same church my parents attended. An old friend from my neighborhood, Tom F., had heard I was clean and trying to get my life in order, so he got my number, gave me a call, and picked me up for a meeting. He was a sight for sore eyes. Tom had been a "hope-to-die" dope fiend, as bad as, or worse than me. At this point he had seven or eight years clean. He took me to many meetings, but his home meeting was First Step. Tom had become a Christian, the real deal. This was short lived for me, however, I wasn't ready yet, I hadn't had enough. This was in the early '90s.

It was to this First Step group that I returned in the summer of 1997 after my stay at the ARC. I returned, done with dope and booze, and surrendered to God. I was now ready to receive what First Step, and more importantly, what God had to offer.

One more thing about Tom, it was he who introduced me to Karen, a wonderful gal who would eventually agree to be my bride. When we first met in the early '90s she was divorced and I was married. When we again met in the fall of 1997, I was divorced, and Karen's second marriage was coming to an end.

23

Finding My Way Back

I'm clean and sober, and firmly heading in the right direction. What now? What do I do? I had now come out of the prison of addiction after serving a twenty-eight-year term. During those years I had, from time to time, experienced brief periods of freedom only to be drawn back into the vortex of addiction.

I was now free. It felt different this time. It <u>was</u> different. There was a surefootedness I had not known before. I had settled the God thing. My insistence on control and the final word was over. I had finally become willing to subordinate my will to God's and do things His way. I had finally had enough of doing things my way. It would probably be more accurate to say that I had finally had enough of the emptiness and destruction that were byproducts of doing things my way.

When I was young, I had a paper route. One day I got into an altercation with the older brother of some kids that had started harassing me on my route. I can't call it a fight, because there was no fight. I got my clock cleaned. I was hospitalized with my jaw broken into three pieces. For the next couple of months I subsisted on chocolate and banana milkshakes that I made myself. All the chocolate ice cream I wanted, it was great. As with my addiction, there came a point where what I liked so much left me wanting. I longed for real food. I no longer craved what was not good for me, but I longed for what was truly good and needful for me. This was the place in life I had come to in regard to my addiction.

There is another interesting parallel to my recovery in this story. When it was finally time to cut the wires that held my jaw closed and in place, I could only move my mouth with difficulty. For lack of use, the muscles that would enable me to talk, chew, and eat, had become flaccid, they had lost all strength. To my horror my long-awaited first meal was a mere shadow of what I had anticipated. I had to work up to even chewing bread. Now, newly clean and sober, I had begun to realize how ill equipped and unpracticed I had become when it came to dealing with the realities. Before my addiction, I knew how to do things and how to navigate polite society; now newly sober, many things had to be relearned.

The purpose of recovery meetings escapes most people. We go to meetings to find community and support from those best equipped to give it, others on the same recovery journey. It is also our school, our classroom. This is a place where we listen for God's words of encouragement and instruction to us. It is also where we take our first shaky steps in a sober world. Like a toddler first learning to walk, it is in this community that we stumble, hit our heads on the coffee table, or tumble down an unguarded flight of stairs. We learn to navigate in an independent and interdependent way, this new and forgotten world we once occupied before addiction. You will hear it said, "To succeed in recovery, you must change your playmates and your playpen." Our meetings are the first step in this process.

24

Making the Switch

It was at about the five-month mark that I made the transition from my traditional AA and NA meetings, three to four a week, to First Step Recovery once a week. Recovery is a process, and had it not been for those traditional meetings, and the richness of all I received there, I would not have been prepared for this move. Recovery is a developmental process. We take one step, then the next, each step preparing us for the next. I am not referring here to the "12 steps," that's another matter.

My history with the church had left me with a bad taste in my mouth, so this move to First Step, which was Christ-centered recovery, was not completely carefree. I didn't have a problem with God, He and I were cool; it was his kids I didn't think much of. And in that regard, not so much individually, but corporately, as a whole. To be quite blunt, I thought they were a bunch of limp-wristed sissies. The folks in AA and NA were my kind of people and I had a great deal of respect for them; the jury was out on these new folks at First Step.

As I continued to apply the principles of the 12 steps to my life, there was an ever-increasing sense of wholeness. There was also a greater sense of stability in my recovery. Although there was much wreckage to be dealt with, life was good and steadily getting better.

It was in addressing the accumulated wreckage of twenty-eight years of poor choices and bad behavior that I came to understand the phrase, "one day at a time." As I looked at this mountain it became overwhelming. I was like a child standing before Mt. Everest. What I learned to do was take one rock at a time, and only one, and I never looked too long at the whole pile. There was a question that was posed to me, that I now ask those I work with who have great obstacles before them, and that is, "How do you eat an elephant?" The answer is, "One bite at a time."

I have come to understand that there are two kinds of miracles, sudden and progressive. I had always wanted God to "poof" me, to suddenly and miraculously fix and change me. That didn't happen. Then there are progressive miracles. This is the miracle that comes about as we walk a situation out, where the hand of God is quietly and subtly at work. A prime example of this is "the feeding of the five thousand" in the Bible. In the story, five loaves and two fish became enough to feed over five thousand people. The miracle took place as they followed Jesus' instructions and began serving what they had. It was in the midst of the process that the miracle happened; what they had was multiplied to become enough to meet the need. In recovery, it is when we apply the God principles of the 12 steps to our lives, and begin to do things God's way, that we begin seeing miracles in our lives. It is as we walk out our recovery God's way that we begin to see the impossible take shape.

I was able to come early to First Step, make the coffee, and set up the book table. This enabled me to make a contribution and helped me to become "a part of."

There is a neat saying I heard from an "old-timer" in AA, and that is, "God is in the ashtrays." What that refers to is this: first off, in the old days you could smoke in a meeting. That meant as part of the setup for a meeting, ashtrays would need to be set out and then afterward be cleaned and put away until they were needed again. Translation: the blessing of God is in the service to others. This is a basic tenet of 12 step recovery.

As time went on, I really found my niche, and I was loving it. I found more to do and the CD (chemical dependency) group was a good place for me. Like so many years earlier, I had again found my people. These Christian recovery folk were OK.

25

Some Wonderful Discoveries

I have come to see the whole "God thing" much differently. Coming to God through the recovery process and not the church has given me a different perspective.

Growing up in the religious tradition I did; it was always about being good enough, measuring up, and doing enough. Under those standards I never knew where I stood with God, but with all the bad I did, I believed I was probably bound for hell. I remember thinking my only hope was if I were killed as I came out of church, right after confession and getting forgiven. One other scenario that had a glimmer of hope for me was that when I got old I would do right for a few years before I died, certainly I could be good when I got old. All the old people I knew looked like they were being good.

In many ways the latter is what happened. At age forty-four, which is not as old as I had envisioned, I had gotten a bellyful of my own ways. It was somewhat like overeating. Have you ever eaten so much that you feel sick and throwing up actually would be welcomed? That was me, not another bite, I was done.

Having come to God through the halls of recovery, and not the church, I came to see God as my rescuer. This was so different from what I grew up with. I experienced God as merciful, and over the years have learned by experience that He truly cares.

I learned that "we all got stuff." I was no worse than anyone else; the dirt in my life was just more visible. We don't get cleaned up, and then come to Him, we come dirty, raggedy, and busted up, just as we are. It is God who, in ways we can not often explain, begins to clean us up, bringing order and healing to our lives. The bad things that once had such a hold on us and held such a prominent place in our lives, begin to fade into the background.

I had a request of God at the beginning. I didn't want to lose the use of a particular four-letter word. My reasoning, as I explained to Him, was simple. It was a word with great versatility, it could add emphasis as no other word in the English language, depending on the context and the tone in which it is used. What happened amazed me, and showed me so much about God. I never felt that I was not allowed to use the word, but what I experienced was so cool. As I continued on this God path, when I did use this word it was ill fitting and distasteful. Consequently I used it less, and over time it seemed to just fall away. I had changed. Surrender to God had brought about an internal change in me. Coming to God would not mean a confining loss of freedom and a bunch of "have-tos," but freedom and a bunch of "get-tos." Doing right was becoming doable.

I have come to understand that God's intent and desire, in everything He would have me set aside, is to bring me into a place of greater and greater liberty. As the weeks, months, and years pass, I experience a greater and greater level of freedom. The ever-increasing freedom I refer to is not the freedom from drugs and alcohol, but freedom from the insecurities, fears, and wounds that made medicating myself a good idea to begin with. The by-product of this freedom is peace. It is a wonderful thing to be at peace with God, but I believe it is an even greater miracle to be at peace with myself.

God is so cool; He has never forced me to become someone I'm not. I do, however, have a strong desire to please Him, and this includes not doing those things I know displease Him. I did not have to become a suit-wearing, Bible-toting square, and hang out with boring people I have nothing in common with. In Christ-centered recovery groups I'm able to run with people like me. We are all, for the most part, on the God path, or considering it as an option.

I have also learned something about the "squares" in the church. First, they have stuff too. They have hurts, struggles, disappointments, and pain, just like me. On the inside, we are the same. The difference is in how they have chosen to walk out their stuff.

This God path can be compared to taking a mud-encrusted truck to a car wash. Little by little, as it goes along, the layers of mud are first softened, then appropriate pressure is applied with different brushes and water jets to remove the layers of caked on dirt. The process is designed to remove only the dirt and in the process not to harm any part of the vehicle or its finish. The end product is a truck free of the excess weight it had accumulated, and now able to be enjoyed as originally intended. That is God's plan for us, to free us from the mud and muck we have accumulated. This includes what we have heaped on ourselves and that which has been slung on us by others. God does not want to lay a bunch of heavy stuff on us, but His desire is to <u>free us</u> so we can be and possess all that He has intended for us.

26

In Conclusion

A s I look back over my life's journey thus far I am able to see myself as a rich and fortunate man, rich in that this journey has carved deep character lines into my face, and fortunate in that I survived. In addition, and probably most importantly, I have experienced firsthand the mercy and grace of God.

The way that I chose to navigate my teen years was not all that uncommon for those turbulent years of the '60s. Many in my generation were ravaged by the effects of the emerging drug culture. Now, in my midfifties, I look back over those years and remember the many whose lives were cut short, and those whose futures were forever altered for the worse. It saddens me. I have come to see myself as a veteran and a fortunate survivor, not of the military, or any military campaign, but a survivor and veteran of a war against a generation, my generation.

I disagree with the old adage, "What doesn't kill you, makes you stronger." Pain and adversity can eventually crush and destroy, and over time, hope is then lost; a life devoid of hope is a heartbreaking thing to experience or observe.

I am grateful for those years and would not trade them away. They have shaped me into the man I am today, and have given me the view of humanity I have today, one of compassion and empathy for the wounded. Most importantly, it was this path that brought me to the end of myself and to the place of recognizing my need for God. It takes what it takes for each of us and for me that was what it took.

I regret deeply the pain and suffering I have caused for so many. My greatest regret to this day is the pain I have caused my daughters by not being the father they needed me to be. God is able to bring good out of the ashes, and my greatest heartfelt prayer is to in every way be a blessing to them now.

Wherever you find yourself in your own life's journey, I encourage you, if you have not already, to surrender your life to God, and allow Him to put the broken pieces of your life back together. I promise you, you will never regret your decision to let go and let God do for you what you are unable to do for yourself.

Surrender truly is The Way Out.

27

Photo Album

Mom and Dad

The home I grew up in.

My sister Deonn and I on the tricycle I left home on.

I never could have imagined what was to come, age 10.

First rehab, DAPC Santa Cruz, California.

Back home from rehab in Santa Cruz, age 18.

Just home from road camp. Me, sister Deonn,
and cousin Vicki, age 19.

Me with my truck, age 20.

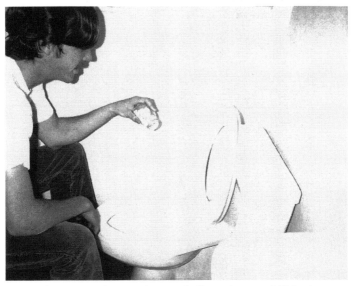

Giving up a drug stash in trade for seeing my girlfriend
before going to probation mandated rehab, age 20.

Dad and I at vacation house in Cayucos, California.
I had just come out of a horrendous home detox, age 28.

In the Duffy Room at Schick Shadel Hospital.
This was staged and done during a follow-up stay, age 29.

Dad and I after Schick on vacation trip to San Diego, age 29.

Daughter Leah and I at her birthday party, age 30.

Daughter Angela and I during Easter visit, age 31.

Enjoying the river, a cigarette, and a glass of vodka, age 34.

My cat Keelia and I both nodded-out on the couch, age 37.

Leah and I at a barbecue, age 38.

Dad and I at Angela's wedding, age 39.

By my shop where I often shot dope and
would be left alone, age 42.

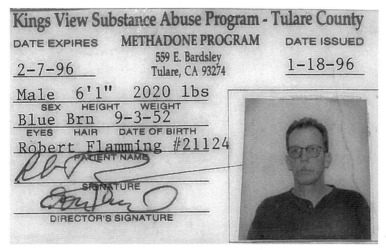

Methadone program ID card, age 43.

Wife Karen and I today.

If you would like to contact the author you may do so by going to:

www.robflammang.com

Or you may write to: Rob Flammang
                     PO Box 7958
                     Visalia, CA 93290-7958